# THE NATURAL AQUARIUM

## How to Imitate Nature in your Home

by Satoshi Yoshino and Doshin Kobayashi
TS-195

| CUSTOMARY U.S. MEASURES AND EQUIVALENTS | | | METRIC MEASURES AND EQUIVALENTS | | |
|---|---|---|---|---|---|
| **LENGTH** | | | | | |
| 1 inch (in) | | = 2.54 cm | 1 millimeter (mm) | | = .0394 in |
| 1 foot (ft) | = 12 in | = .3048 m | 1 centimeter (cm) | = 10 mm | = .3937 in |
| 1 yard (yd) | = 3 ft | = .9144 m | 1 meter (m) | = 1000 mm | = 1.0936 yd |
| 1 mile (mi) | = 1760 yd | = 1.6093 km | 1 kilometer (km) | = 1000 m | = .6214 mi |
| 1 nautical mile | = 1.152 mi | = 1.853 km | | | |
| **AREA** | | | | | |
| 1 square inch (in²) | | = 6.4516 cm² | 1 sq centimeter (cm²) | = 100 mm² | = .155 in² |
| 1 square foot (ft²) | = 144 in² | = .093 m² | 1 sq meter (m²) | = 10,000 cm² | = 1.196 yd² |
| 1 square yard (yd²) | = 9 ft² | = .8361 m² | 1 hectare (ha) | = 10,000 m² | = 2.4711 acres |
| 1 acre | = 4840 yd² | = 4046.86 m² | 1 sq kilometer (km²) | = 100 ha | = .3861 mi² |
| 1 square mile( mi²) | = 640 acre | = 2.59 km² | | | |
| **WEIGHT** | | | | | |
| 1 ounce (oz) | = 437.5 grains | = 28.35 g | 1 milligram (mg) | | = .0154 grain |
| 1 pound (lb) | = 16 oz | = .4536 kg | 1 gram (g) | = 1000 mg | = .0353 oz |
| 1 short ton | = 2000 lb | = .9072 t | 1 kilogram (kg) | = 1000 g | = 2.2046 lb |
| 1 long ton | = 2240 lb | = 1.0161 t | 1 tonne (t) | = 1000 kg | = 1.1023 short tons |
| | | | 1 tonne | | = .9842 long ton |
| **VOLUME** | | | | | |
| 1 cubic inch (in³) | | = 16.387 cm³ | 1 cubic centimeter (cm³) | | = .061 in³ |
| 1 cubic foot (ft³) | = 1728 in³ | = .028 m³ | 1 cubic decimeter (dm³) | = 1000 cm³ | = .353 ft³ |
| 1 cubic yard (yd³) | = 27 ft³ | = .7646 m³ | 1 cubic meter (m³) | = 1000 dm³ | = 1.3079 yd³ |
| | | | 1 liter (l) | = 1 dm³ | = .2642 gal |
| 1 fluid ounce (fl oz) | | = 2.957 cl | 1 hectoliter (hl) | = 100 l | = 2.8378 bu |
| 1 liquid pint (pt) | = 16 fl oz | = .4732 l | | | |
| 1 liquid quart (qt) | = 2 pt | = .946 l | | | |
| 1 gallon (gal) | = 4 qt | = 3.7853 l | | | |
| 1 dry pint | | = .5506 l | | | |
| 1 bushel (bu) | = 64 dry pt | = 35.2381 l | | | |

## TEMPERATURE

$$CELSIUS° = 5/9 \ (F° - 32°) \quad FAHRENHEIT° = 9/5 \ C° + 32°$$

**Photographers:** Dr. Herbert R. Axelrod, K.L. Chew, Dr. H.-J. Franke, B. Kahl, Doshin Kobayashi, H. Linke, M.P. & C. Piednoir, H.-J. Richter, A. Roth, S. Shubel, W. Sommer, A. van den Nieuwenhuizen, Lo Wing Yat, Satoshi Yoshino, R. Zuka

This book was originally published in Japanese under the title *AQUATIC SCENE*. It was subsequently translated into the German language and edited to be suitable for that market. The German edition was translated by U.Erich Friese, General Curator, Sydney (Darling Harbour) Aquarium, Sydney, Australia. This edition was then edited by Dr. Herbert R. Axelrod to bring it up to date.

© German Edition, 1991 bede Verlag, W-8371 Kollnburg, Germany
All rights reserved. Publisher and authors cannot be held liable for damages sustained from changes made by the editors.

Translated from the Japanese book called *AQUATIC SCENE* by Satoshi Yoshino and Doshin Kobayashi, Marine Planning Co.,Ltd.Tokyo, Japan

### 1996 Edition

987654321                                                                                                    95  789

Distributed in the UNITED STATES to the Pet Trade by T.F.H. Publications, Inc., One T.F.H. Plaza, Neptune City, NJ 07753; distributed in the UNITED STATES to the Bookstore and Library Trade by National Book Network, Inc. 4720 Boston Way, Lanham MD 20706; in CANADA to the Pet Trade by H & L Pet Supplies Inc., 27 Kingston Crescent, Kitchener, Ontario N2B 2T6; Rolf C. Hagen Inc., 3225 Sartelon St. Laurent-Montreal Quebec H4R 1E8; in CANADA to the Book Trade by Vanwell Publishing Ltd., 1 Northrup Crescent, St. Catharines, Ontario L2M 6P5 ; in ENGLAND by T.F.H. Publications, PO Box 15, Waterlooville PO7 6BQ; in AUSTRALIA AND THE SOUTH PACIFIC by T.F.H. (Australia), Pty. Ltd., Box 149, Brookvale 2100 N.S.W., Australia; in NEW ZEALAND by Brooklands Aquarium Ltd. 5 McGiven Drive, New Plymouth, RD1 New Zealand; in Japan by T.F.H. Publications, Japan—Jiro Tsuda, 10-12-3 Ohjidai, Sakura, Chiba 285, Japan; in SOUTH AFRICA by Lopis (Pty) Ltd., P.O. Box 39127, Booysens, 2016, Johannesburg, South Africa. Published by T.F.H. Publications, Inc.
MANUFACTURED IN THE UNITED STATES OF AMERICA
BY T.F.H. PUBLICATIONS, INC.

# TABLE OF CONTENTS

# 1

# WATER PLANTS THE WORLD OVER

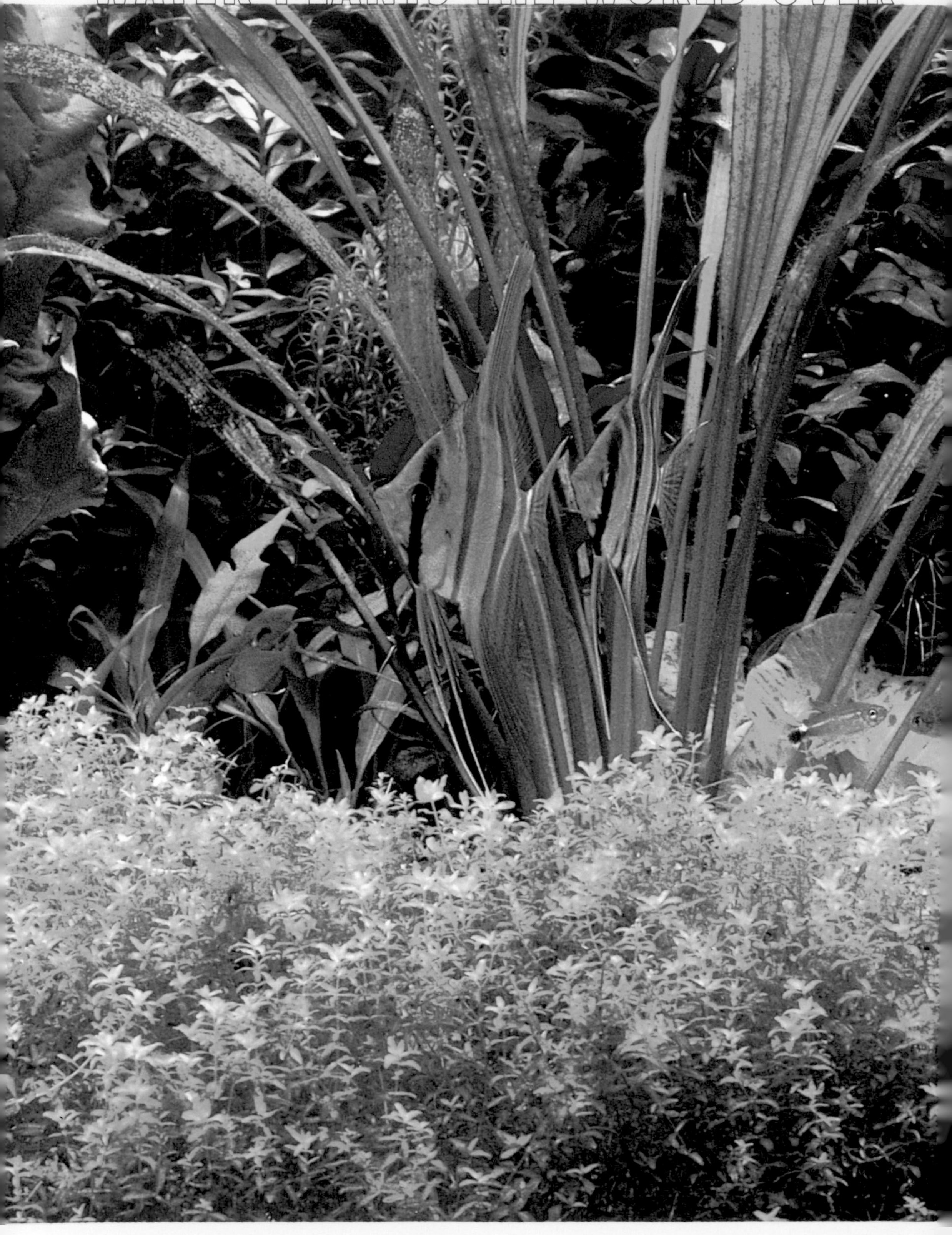

This book will show that various types of water plants can indeed thrive in an aquarium if they have been correctly selected and are properly cared for. Here we are talking about dynamic underwater landscapes that look like miniature pieces of nature transplanted into an aquarium. In these "scapes," composed of wild growing water plants, rocks and driftwood, fishes are exhibited to make the aquascape more realistic. In the so-called Dutch Aquariums the plants are foremost, while the fishes, if indeed the aquarium contains any, are secondary. In the natural aquarium, the fishes and plants have equal importance.

Anyone who sees an aquarium like this will become enchanted immediately. Various examples of how to aesthetically achieve this will be discussed in the following chapters. Also given are detailed data and methods on how to arrange the various display components. In those aquaria where plants are the focal point of attention, culturing the plants becomes the most important task at hand. Even when nicely grown plants are available and these are then used in the aquascaping process, it can still happen that such plants—the basis of any aquarium underwater landscaping method—will not grow and they slowly disintegrate. These so-called "dying aquariums" are indeed sad displays. It must always be remembered that all plants and fishes in an aquarium are alive and this should be clearly visible; to achieve this is one of the objectives of this book.

A thriving aquascaped aquarium reflects the fullest measure of nature's harmony.

In tanks where the plants are growing well, the aquarium environment becomes stabilized and consequently the fish will display their best coloration. Many aquarists long for the tropics and would dearly like to visit the habitats of the plants and fishes which they commonly keep in their tanks. The reality though is very much different from what we imagine it to be. Generally, those combinations of plants and fishes commonly kept by aquarists rarely ever occur in nature. What aquarium displays really depict are only aquarium "scenes" or "aquascapes." They convey pictures of plants and fishes living together. In most cases the plants and fishes kept in the aquarium are never found together in nature.

In a natural-appearing aquarium scene we not only focus on living plants and fishes, but also on other components such as driftwood, rocks and bottom substrate. Since these are all essential display elements it is important to use only those which look "natural." Anyone can get them; a walk to the appropriate natural environment or to the nearest aquarium shop will do. For instance, a bit of genuine river sand sprinkled over the sand purchased from the local pet shop tends to create a more natural appearance. We would indeed be happy if this book with its examples provides encouragement to aquarists to set up natural looking aquariums.

Aquarists who are purists and want to design an actual piece of underwater nature, are invited to create what is called a "biotope aquarium." A wonderful book has been written about this subject by Werner Stawikowski and it is called *The Biotope Aquarium* (T.F.H. publication TT-026). In the biotope aquarium only plants, stones, twigs and fishes actually found together in nature are acceptable.

The purist will not be content with creating a
pretty aquarium, but will constantly strive to
duplicate the natural environment of the fishes
he is keeping.

Each species of plant and fish in this fabulous aquarium was carefully chosen for compatibility. The effect is stunning!

DATA

*Water temperature*: 25°C (77°F).

*Tank dimensions*: 150 x 50 x 50 cm (60 x 20 x 20 in.) all-glass tank.

*Illumination*: 3 x 40-watt lamps.

*Influx of daylight*: None.

*Bottom substrate*: gravel.

*Filtration*: Inside filter.

*Water changes*: ⅓ of tank volume once per week.

*Heating*: 200-watt heater, thermostatically controlled.

*Fertilizer*: Plant fertilizer mixed in; liquid fertilizer added with water change. Addition of carbon dioxide via diffuser pipe.

*Water quality*: pH 6.8; hardness (total) 8° DH (German units).

*Carbon dioxide in solution*: 16 mg per liter.

In this magnificent water–plant arrangement, the various colors and shapes create an aesthetically pleasant contrast. Even the height of individual plants is deliberately controlled; not by trimming back the tall runners of the plants in the front, but instead by taking advantage of the natural growth of different plant species. Therefore, natural maximum height differences of various plants lead to a natural plant growth formation throughout the tank. The foreground of low-growing plants is deliberately created to provide adequate swimming space for the fishes. Due to the luxuriant plant growth, neither the back wall nor the bottom are visible. This creates an appealing feeling of depth. Miniature Tenellus and dwarf *Sagittaria* grow in the foreground.

In contrast to common aquarium decorating practices, neither rocks nor driftwood are used here. The aesthetics of this tank are created solely by water plants.

Similar to the water plant selection criteria listed above, selecting fish should also be done on the basis of contrast. We select fish that may be similar in body shape but not in coloration.

Even such hard-to-please fish as discus can be kept in such a densely planted tank. The large number of water plants assures a stable equilibrium of the aquarium in terms of water chemistry, living fishes and functional plants.

### SETTING UP THE TANK

A tank length of 120 cm (48 in.) is considered to be the minimum size for a tank for this display. Only this size range offers sufficient flexibility for an imaginative "aquascaping" with water plants.

The primary objective is to achieve optimum plant growth. Therefore, plant fertilizer is added to the substrate. The lighting requires similar detailed attention. A minimum of three to four fluorescent

1 Hygrophila difformis
2 Hygrophila angustifolia
3 Cryptocoryne usteriana
4 Ludwigia palustris
5 Didiplis diandra
6 Echinodorus quadricostatus
7 Ludwigia repens x palustris
8 Gymnocoronis spilanthoides
9 Cryptocoryne pontederiifolia
10 Cryptocoryne walkeri
11 Cryptocoryne petchii
12 Shinnersia rivulatus
13 Rotala wallichii
14 Heteranthera zosterifolia
15 Alternanthera sessilis var. rubra
16 Nymphaea lotus
17 Ammania senegalensis
18 Echinodorus tenellus
19 Cryptocoryne balansae
20 Rotala rotundifolia
21 Hygrophila stricta
22 Alternanthera sessilis var.
   lilacina
23 Cryptocoryne wendtii

24 Sagittaria subulata var. pusilla
25 Hottonia palustris
26 Vallisneria spiralis
27 Cryptocoryne affinis
28 Echinodorus parviflorus
29 Riccia fluitans

30 Hygrophila polysperma
31 Rotala macrantha
32 Hemianthus micranthemoides
33 Alternanthera sessilis
34 Limnophila aquatica
35 Mayaca vandellii

Apistogramma nijsseni
Caridina sp.

Symphysodon aequifasciatus
Otocinclus arnoldi

Megalamphodus sweglesi
Megalamphodus megalopterus

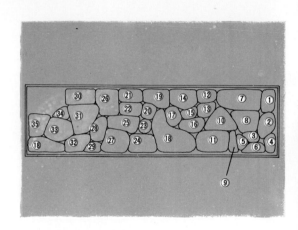

## SELECTING THE FISHES

For the middle and upper water layers we select active swimmers such as the two phantom tetras, *Megalamphodus sweglesi* and *M. megalopterus*. *Otocinclus arnoldi* will continuously graze over the plants, feeding on thin algal threads, and thus assure the optical cleanliness of the aquarium. The dwarf cichlid *Apistogramma nijsseni,* with its calm swimming motions represents an eye-pleasing contrast to the active tetras. Medium-size, healthy discus then complete the picture. We can further add bottom-dwelling catfish of the genus *Corydoras*. Even delicate freshwater shrimp could be kept in such a water-plant aquarium.

*Corydoras melanistus* is a shy little fish that will feel safe and secure in the well-planted aquarium.

tubes of 30 or 40 watts each will be required. When planting the tank, we start out at the back with the uncomplicated stemmed plants. After a week or so the water in the tank will have stabilized, and then we can plant the foreground. At that stage we can also introduce the first few fish. The accompanying illustrations show a relatively large number of *Cryptocoryne* ; these are not planted until after the tank has been in operation for a month. It is important that the plants are thinned out regularly. Partial water changes and artificial carbon dioxide supplements have a strong influence on plant growth.

In order to maintain the beauty of a water-plant aquarium it is advisable to assess overall plant growth. Prune the plants with a scissors as needed.

This depicts a creation that emphasizes the development of stemmed water plants. The highly-developed art of rearing water plants is confirmed by the impression and splendor of this underwater landscape. On one hand this is achieved through plant arrangement, which takes into account the contrast between red and green plants, and on the other hand by adding many so-called *difficult* plants.

Planting proceeds as already discussed for stemmed plants. Those species that grow faster than others are placed along the back of the tank; slow-growing plants go into the foreground. Because of different growth rates of the various species,

we achieve natural height differences in the optical appearance of the tank. The use of different and dissimilarly-shaped plant species creates aesthetic variety. This then emphasizes the characteristics of individual plants, as well as color contrasts between the plants. Red and green plants are, of course, planted alternately. In arranging the plants we also consider various shades of green. Such deliberate structuring of plant arrangements creates a splendid picture for the viewer. This is further enhanced by the movements of differently shaped and colored fishes in the tank. We select fishes which frequent various water zones. As color splashes we

# WITH WATER PLANTS

DATA
*Water temperature*: 24°C (76°F).
*Tank dimensions:* 120 x 60 x 60 cm (48 x 24 x 24 in.) all-glass tank.
*Lighting:* 2 x 30-watt bulbs and 2 x 15-watt bulbs; daily illumination period 12 hours.
*Influence of daylight:* Up to midday.
*Substrate:* Coarse beach or river sand.
*Filtration:* External filtration system.
*Water changes:* ⅓ of total volume once per week.
*Heating*: 200-watt heater.
*Fertilizer*: Addition of plant fertilizer, depending upon condition of plants.
*Water quality:* pH 6.8.
*Carbonate hardness:*6° DH.
*Carbon dioxide in solution*: 10 mg.

introduce *Rasbora heteromorpha* from Southeast Asia, and for perpetual motion we use various *Xiphophorus* (swordtail) and tetra species. These fishes get along well with each other and together with the plants they form a beautiful picture.

This dream tank is maintained by carefully and artistically trimming small pieces off the plants as necessary to keep them from overgrowing the tank.

1 *Vallisneria spiralis* forma *tortifolia*
2 *Lagarosiphon major*
3 *Cardamine lyrata*
4 *Hydrocotyle leucopetala*
5 *Cryptocoryne petchii*
6 *Hemianthus micranthemoides*
7 *Aglaodorum griffithii*
8 *Cabomba piauhyensis*
9 *Mayaca vandelli*

10 *Alternanthera sessilis* var. *lilacina*
11 *Hottonia palustris*
12 *Echinodorus quadricostatus*
13 *Hygrophila stricta*
14 *Cryptocoryne balansae*
15 *Ludwigia repens x palustris*
16 *Dysophylla verticillata*
17 *Lobelia cardinalis*

18 *Echinodorus tenellus*
19 *Heteranthera zosterifolia*
20 *Drymaria cordata*
21 *Didiplis diandra*
22 *Saururus cernuus*
23 *Alternanthera sessilis*
24 *Limnophila aquatica*
25 *Bacopa monniera*

*Colisa lalia*

*Nannostomus trifasciatus*

*Xiphophorus variatus*

14

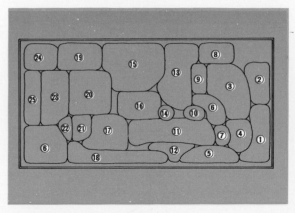

## SETTING UP THE TANK

When decorating an aquarium with long-stemmed water plants it is advisable to purchase a tank of at least 90 cm (36 in.) length. The thoroughly washed sand is spread out over the bottom in a layer of 3 to 5 cm (1 to 2 in.) deep.

Plants to be used should include those difficult to grow indoors, such as *Dysophylla verticillata*. In order to rear these kinds of water plants we should take advantage of available natural light. Consequently, this sort of tank should be located so that it receives gentle, indirect light in the morning and artificial illumination in the afternoon. This way the water plants will get the required light. Total output of the artificial illumination should be about 90 watts.

## CARING FOR THE WATER PLANTS

Water changes are very important for water plants and this should be done on a weekly basis. New minerals should be added to the water with each partial replacement.

Carbon dioxide supplementation must be viewed as an important aid to proper plant growth. The combination of water changes together with carbon dioxide supplements facilitates the growth of even "difficult" plant species. If,

however, water changes cannot be made weekly, daily and closely controlled supplements of carbon dioxide are essential.

If the aquarium is positioned in such a way that we can take advantage of natural light during the early part of the day, artificial lighting will only be necessary during the afternoon. Preferably such a lighting regimen should be controlled by a timer switch. In the tank shown on this page, all stemmed plants are planted closely together. Since they virtually cover the entire substrate it will be difficult to trim the plants in the back half of the tank. In this case it is better to trim about one-third of the planted area at the same time. Trimming removes all runners that have moved out too far. At first, shorten the lower parts of the plants in the back and so control the height of their stems. Then the plants farther toward the front are treated the same way.

If all of the plants have become too tall, about half of them are removed and stored in a separate container. Then, the remaining plants are trimmed. Next, the plants that were just taken out are also trimmed (as above) and are then returned to the main tank. The regular shortening of aquarium plants is an important task that must not be neglected. Pruning of water plants is as important as pruning terrestrial plants.

## SELECTING THE FISHES

It is always advisable to select fish that swim at different levels in an aquarium. For instance, there are typical mid-water fishes like zebras and barbs, as well as bottom fishes such as *Corydoras* catfish. Furthermore, it is also useful to keep fish together that exhibit different swimming speeds and behaviors. Barbs and tetras, for instance, are characteristically fast swimmers,

*Aphyocharax rathbuni.* Their jumping tendency will be curtailed in the planted aquarium, but be sure to cover your tank anyway.

*Nannostomus trifasciatus* is a peaceful little tetra with a great fondness for live worms.

*Characidium* sp. spends most of its time hopping from place to place in search of tidbits of food on the bottom of the aquarium.

while the various gourami species (labyrinth fishes) glide very gently and slowly through the aquarium. The aquarium shown here contains a combination of fishes from different continents. Their food requirements are standard and approximately identical. Commercially available types of dry food can sometimes be combined with frozen foods. This provides for a varied and quite adequate diet. Freeze-dried foods, such as mosquito larvae, should be offered to the surface fish that will eagerly feed on it as they swim along the surface. Pelleted foods are much better than flake foods since they do not pollute the water as easily and they feed all the fishes as they slowly sink to the bottom.

Dry and frozen foods that sink slowly toward the bottom are more suitable for occupants of the middle and lower water zones. Therefore, it is imperative to keep the diet varied. Feeding three times daily an amount which is totally eaten within ten minutes is ideal for adult fishes. Juvenile or baby fishes require more frequent feeding.

**FISH SELECTION**

*Aphyocharax rathbuni,* sometimes called the Ruby Tetra—a South American tetra which should be kept in small schools.

*Nannostomus trifasciatus,* Three-banded Pencilfish—a beautiful tetra from the Amazon region, which should also be kept in small groups.

*Characidium fasciatum,* the Darter Characin. Bottom dweller that rests among rocks and driftwood.

*Nannostomus espei*, Espe's Pencilfish, is an attractive tetra that maintains a slightly oblique swimming position.

*Hyphessobrycon heterorhabdus*, the Three-lined Tetra, is also from the Amazon region and therefore prefers softer water.

*Hyphessobrycon herbertaxelrodi*, the Black Flag Tetra. This attractively colored tetra prefers the upper water layers for swimming.

*Xiphophorus variatus.* The platy is hardy, beautiful, and available in a fascinating array of colors and patterns.

*Carnegiella strigata*, the Marbled Hatchetfish, is an interesting fish from the Amazon region with a deep and laterally compressed body. Tank must be covered since these fish tend to jump.

*Nematobrycon* species. The Rainbow Tetra, or Red-eyed Emperor Tetra is a schooling fish with a beautiful metallic sheen.

Marbled Hatchetfish are equipped with very strong pectoral fins that enable them to glide along the surface of the water, snapping up insects as they go.

*Rasbora heteromorpha*, the Rasbora or Harlequin Fish, is a schooling fish from Southeast Asia; very active swimmer.

*Rasbora hengeli*, Hengel's Rasbora. This is a species from Sumatra that looks very similar to the Harlequin Fish.

*Xiphophorus variatus*, a Platy hybrid form. The livebearing platies are well known aquarium fishes that are principally herbivorous (feeding on plant material). They like to graze on algae from plant leaves.

*Colisa lalia*, the Dwarf Gourami. This is a bubblenest builder from India. The male is very colorful. Eggs are deposited in a large bubblenest built near the surface.

*Colisa lalia* are able to live in still waters with low oxygen levels.

DATA
*Water temperature*: 25°C (77°F).
*Tank dimensions*: 120 x 50 x 60 cm (48 x 18 x 24 in.) all-glass tank.
*Lighting:* 1 x 30-watt tube and 1 x 20-watt tube.
*Daily illumination period*: 12 hours.
*Influx of daylight*: None.
*Substrate*: Coarse river sand.
*Filtration:* Inside filter.
*Water change*: ⅓ of tank volume once per week.
*Heating:* 150-watt thermostatically-controlled heater.
*Fertilizer*: Substrate permeated with plant fertilizer. Controlled supplements of fertilizer during water changes.
*Carbon dioxide supplement*: added via diffuser.
*Water quality*: pH 6.9; hardness 4° DH.
*Carbon dioxide in solution*: 10 mg per liter.

This is a tank decorated specifically to focus on the elegant shape and graceful swimming of angelfish, *Pterophyllum* species. The back of the tank is planted with *Vallisneria,* which tend to get tall. These cover up the back wall and still offer adequate swimming space for the angelfish. The foreground as well as the center area of the tank is planted densely with *Echinodorus quadricostatus.* The esthetic effect of this is accentuated by the miniature Amazon swordplants in the foreground and yet there is still adequate swimming area for the majestic angelfish. The latter have large fins, which have a tendency to grow relative to the tank height. For that reason an angelfish tank must have a minimum height of 50 cm, better yet 60 cm.

In order to properly focus on the

*Vallisneria* growth offers adequate hiding places for the other fishes.

Through the large-scale use of *Vallisneria* and *Echinodorus*, with their extreme growth characteristics, the depth (front to back) of the tank depicted on these pages has been enhanced. Even though this particular underwater landscape has been structured very simply, the elegant shape of *Pterophyllum* makes it aesthetically very effective.

## SETTING UP THE TANK

Height and depth are essential for this plant arrangement. For

marvelous body shape of these fish, it is advisable to use those plant species where the leaves grow long and horizontal. *Vallisneria* with its intense green provides an excellent contrast to the light green *Echinodorus*.

Even though *Pterophyllum* are elegant looking fish, they can display a nasty disposition; indeed, angelfish occasionally display severe intra-specific aggression. Once a mated pair has formed, they will search for a spawning site and then fiercely defend it against their own tankmates. Dense

Angelfish are able to weave in and out of the spaces between the long leaves of the *Vallisneria*.

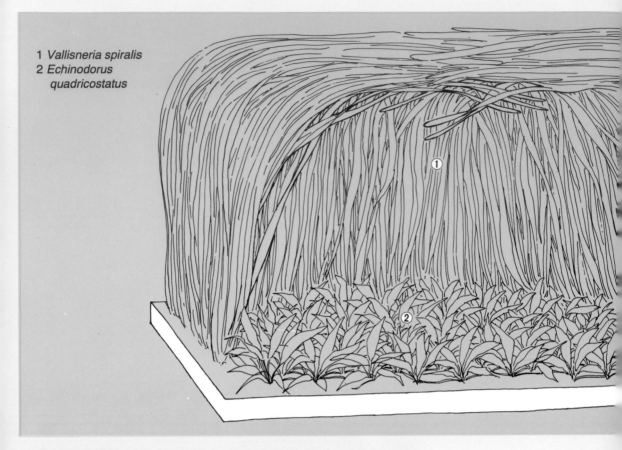

1 *Vallisneria spiralis*
2 *Echinodorus quadricostatus*

*Pterophyllum scalare* variety

*Pterophyllum scalare* variety

*Pterophyllum scalare*

*Pterophyllum scalare* variety

angelfish, which sometimes tend to get very long fins, a tank of about 60 cm in height is desirable. Coarse river sand as well as small pebbles are suitable as bottom substrate. Pebbles have a tendency to brighten up a tank considerably.

River sand facilitates proper plant growth. Since *Echinodorus*, which requires a lot of fertilizer, is also very

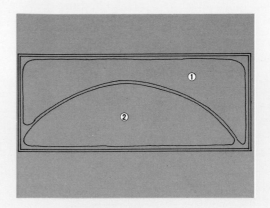

system. Most common systems are commercially available from aquarium shops, where they can be inspected in detail. The inside filter remains hidden behind the dense *Vallisneria* cover. Of course, other filtration systems can also be used. Angelfish prefer clear, soft water. The various angelfish varieties commonly traded these days are not very demanding in care and maintenance.

## SELECTING THE FISHES

*Pterophyllum* are aquarium fish that are being bred commercially in huge quantities with many new varieties appearing each year. A number of color varieties are commonly available. There are also large differences in finnage, and so there are long-finned fish, and those with long-filamentous fins, as well as angelfish with normally developed

labor intensive, it is advisable to mix the plant fertilizer into the substrate at the same time as the plant is placed. The plants will have to be trimmed regularly.*Vallisneria* will form a dense thicket and the swordplants will completely cover the bottom. The latter develop many runners, which should be removed periodically. The most effective aquarium fertilization in modern tropical fishkeeping is carbon dioxide, which is diffused into the aquarium via an airstone or a reactor (contact)

The long, dark leaves of the *Vallisneria* and the short, light leaves of the *Echinodorus* make this a tank of contrast.

21

fins. The basic coloration is silver
with black vertical bands. Fish with
marbled patterns as well as jet-black
fish are also very popular. There are
also color varieties that have an
intense golden coloration on and
around the head, which makes them
highly desirable. *Pterophyllum* grow
very fast, so that you need not have
any hesitation about buying small
specimens. They are aggressive
feeders that will accept almost any
food.

Growth is further enhanced by
feeding a carnivorous diet. Feeding
mosquito larvae is clearly indicated.
Many types of fish food are available
from aquarium shops in frozen form.
Live foods delight them. Flake foods
are not recommended.

Angelfish will spawn in a
community tank. The mated pair
selects a spawning substrate, usually
a large leaf or a sloping rock. The
intended spawning site is then
meticulously cleaned by both fish.
Next, the female deposits a string of
eggs side by side on the spawning
site. The male immediately fertilizes
the eggs. The larvae will hatch in
about 2 days, and after another 2
days the young fish begin to swim
about the tank.

Unfortunately, angelfish will often
eat their own eggs, so that angelfish
breeding without any problems is
really the exception rather than the
rule. If you are determined to raise
angelfish fry successfully, you must
remove the entire clutch after
spawning, transferring the eggs and
the spawning surface to another
(rearing) tank. The rearing tank must
have the same water values as the
main tank. Baby angelfish can easily
be raised with very fine powdered
(dry) food and brine shrimp (*Artemia*)
nauplii.

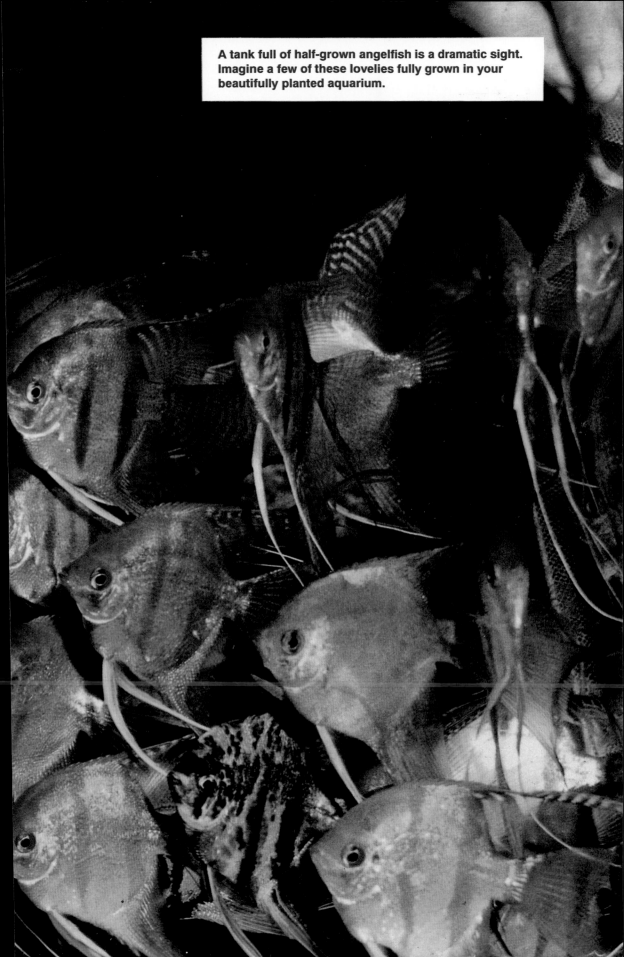

A tank full of half-grown angelfish is a dramatic sight. Imagine a few of these lovelies fully grown in your beautifully planted aquarium.

# COMMUNITY TANK FOR THE KING

Discus are the true kings of the freshwater aquarium; just look at the majestic fishes on these pages. The tank shown is perfectly decorated for them.

By combining dark roots with the fresh green of underwater plants, a magnificent picture has been created. The different discus varieties form a colorful contrast.

In order to be able to secure the plants properly in the substrate, a sand layer of at least 4 cm must be used. Keeping these magnificent fish in a properly decorated tank is unfortunately still an exception these days. Usually discus are still being kept in sterile-looking tanks purely in order to breed them successfully. Yet, it is a lot more fun to care for these fish in a tank as shown here. And even in a tank like this it is quite possible to breed discus. However, rearing the young is admittedly much easier in a sterile tank.

Since this is a tank for discus, it is of paramount importance to arrange for adequate swimming space because they will present themselves in a far more attractive way with open space. To the left and right in the tank we position extra-large roots which are not only attractive but also useful. These roots must be soaked sufficiently and must be properly secured. Heavy and bizarre-looking roots, which fully serve our purpose, are commonly available from large aquarium shops. Under no circumstances can these roots be permitted to get moldy in the tank. Do NOT use roots of unknown origin as they usually contain environmental pollutants extremely

**DATA**
*Water temperature*: 28°C (82°F).
*Tank dimensions*: 180 X 60 X 60 cm (72 x 24 x 24 in.) acrylic tank.
*Lighting*: 2 x 30-watt bulbs, warm white; 2 x 30-watt grow-light bulbs.
*Illumination period*: Daily 12 hours.
*Influx of daylight*: None.
*Substrate*: Coarse river sand or small, dark gravel.
*Filtration*: Outside filter with biochamber.
*Water changes*: Twice weekly, ¼ volume each.
*Heating*: Two 200-watt heaters (thermostatically-controlled).
*Fertilizer*: In consideration of the discus, only small amounts of fertilizer. Regular carbon dioxide supplement via diffuser pipe.
*Water quality*: pH 6.2.
*Carbonate hardness:* 3°DH.
*Carbon dioxide in solution:* 10 mg per liter.

Discus are happiest when they know they have a safe retreat. The plants will cushion them from injuring themselves on the glass if they do take a wild dash around the tank.

1 *Heteranthera zosterifolia*    5 *Echinodorus amazonicus*
2 *Bacopa monnieri*              6 *Echinodorus quadricostatus*
3 *Aponogeton ulvaceus*         7 *Vallisneria spiralis*
4 *Echinodorus osiris*          8 *Mayaca vandelli*

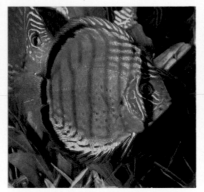

*S. aequifasciatus aequifasciatus*
*Symphysodon aequifasciatus* var.

*Symphysodon aequifasciatus* var.
*Symphysodon aequifasciatus* var.

dangerous to all fishes...especially discus.

Best suited for a tall discus tank are rosette-shaped plants that do not need too much light. Plants that will grow easily and can stand high water temperatures are ideal for this purpose. The tall water plants accentuate the shape of the driftwood, and the rosette-shaped, miniature plants in the foreground emphasize the height of the roots. It is important that plant growth in a discus aquarium is healthy, because these plants remove large amounts of nitrogenous waste, such as ammonia, from the water. Plants that are in good condition assure favorable water conditions for fish; however, if plants grow poorly it also has negative effects on the fish. For instance, if leaves start to decompose, the nitrogenous waste increases and as a consequence the discus will suffer.

## SETTING UP THE TANK

The tank shown is 180 x 60 x 60 cm (72 x 24 x 24 in.) but smaller tanks like 120 x 50 x 50 cm are also suitable. The bottom is covered with washed sand or gravel. Since the bottom of the aquarium is not completely covered with plants, plant fertilizer is only mixed into the substrate at certain sites. When roots are used it is important to remember that tannic acid can leach from the wood into the water. For that reason roots must always be thoroughly soaked. Acidification of the water does not present a problem; however, roots that start to get covered in mold and fungus can be dangerous. Therefore, you should smell the wet roots as well as the aquarium water. Discus are rather sensitive to tannic acid and to decomposing substances in the water. If discus are not feeling well, they will become discolored and turn dark.

With a view towards breeding the delicate discus, large capacity filters should be installed on such a tank. It is important that the water does not become too turbulent from the filter discharge. Discus do not like strong currents. It is therefore advisable to discharge the filter return back into the tank via a spray bar, through many small holes.

With regard to lighting, it is important to make sure that even the small plants along the bottom get sufficient light. Any deficiency here will be compensated for through carbon dioxide fertilization. Discus can easily be kept in normally

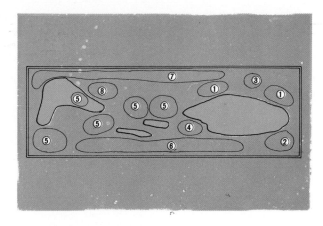

illuminated aquariums. It is incorrect to state that discus only tolerate subdued lighting.

## SELECTING THE PLANTS

Plants selected for this sort of tank must be easy to grow and be able to tolerate high water temperatures. In

Your discus will show their full colors in the stress-free environment of the planted aquarium.

the back of the tank, we plant *Vallisneria spiralis* and *Heteranthera zoster i folia* to complement the roots. The foreground is covered with *Echinodorus amazonicus* and *Echinodorus quadricostatus*. In their native Amazon habitat, discus prefer to remain along overgrown river banks with tree roots protruding into the water. Among the many large plants are the bushy-looking *Mayaca vandelii*. These convey a fresh impression and they do well in high water temperatures.

Regular water changes are welcomed by both fish and plants. Only the stemmed plants are trimmed, but not until the tips of their leaves start to lay on the water's surface. Should the plants become discolored and start to die off, a bit of substrate fertilizer should be added.

**SELECTING THE FISHES**

Discus can be placed into this tank as juveniles, but rearing them is not

The water quality in the planted discus aquarium is enhanced by the plants' ability to remove the nitrates from the water.

Discus often prefer to spawn on the broad leaves of plants.

easy. Small discus must be fed at least four to six times daily. Leftover food must always be siphoned out immediately in order to avoid the formation of decomposition products in the water. Nitrate values in excess of 50 mg/liter must be avoided.

It is better to introduce half-grown discus of about 6-months of age into this tank; the total length of such fish is about 10 to 11 cm (4 in.) measured from the tip of snout to the end of the tail. Healthy discus are light colored and feed eagerly. They must never appear frightened. It goes without saying that you can also use adult discus for such a tank.

Discus are available in different color varieties. Selection depends very much on individual taste and available funds. Much aquarium literature is available that can provide further help and information in regard to keeping and breeding these kings of the aquarium.

An aquarium of 60 cm (24 in.) in length, densely planted with *Ceratopteris thalicroides*, is quite suitable for adult guppies (any variety). For decorative purposes, the accompanying photograph shows only males of the various strains; however, breeding the different guppy strains should always be done in a separate breeding tank, using 2 males and 5 females.

Adult guppies, especially the females, tend to eat their own progeny. This tendency is particularly strong among the various line-bred varieties.

Water plants with fine, branched leaves match the delicate beauty of the pastel-colored guppies. In order to further enhance the glorious coloration of male guppies, only a single type of water plant species has been used in the tank shown here. As you can see for yourself, there is a certain charm in such simplicity. This plant species is ideal for a guppy aquarium. It grows well in an aquarium and must be suitably trimmed at regular intervals. It continues to thrive even in cold water, and so it is clearly the plant of choice for a guppy display. In the tank shown here, the large runners were planted in the back and the shorter ones in the foreground of the tank. Initially, the number of plants

DATA
*Water temperature:* 25°C (77°F).
*Tank dimensions:* 60 x 30 x 36 cm (24 x 12 x 14 in.) all-glass tank.
*Lighting:* 2 x 20-watt warm light tubes.
*Daily illumination* = 12 hours.
*Influx of daylight:* up to midday only.
*Substrate:* Coarse sand or small gravel.
*Filtration:* Undergravel filter.
*Water changes:* ⅓ of tank volume once per week.
*Heating:* 1 x 100-watt heater (thermostatically controlled).
*Fertilizer:* None.
*Water quality:* pH 7.2.
*Carbonate hardness:* 6°DH
*Carbon dioxide in solution:* 6 mg per liter.

Guppies are prolific livebearers, but are also cannibals that eat their young at any opportunity. The fine leaves of the plants provide many safe havens for the newborn fry. In a tank of this kind, you will eventually have many generations of guppies with a very stable population.

in the foreground should be kept down, because the larger plants in the back will quickly grow runners that creep into the foreground. In this way, a magnificent underwater landscape will be established in a very short period of time.

## SETTING UP THE TANK

The size of a guppy aquarium is not too important; however, an aquarium of about 60 cm (24 in.) maximum dimension is quite suitable for that purpose. If a large tank is being used, the height should not exceed 45 cm (18 in.) since

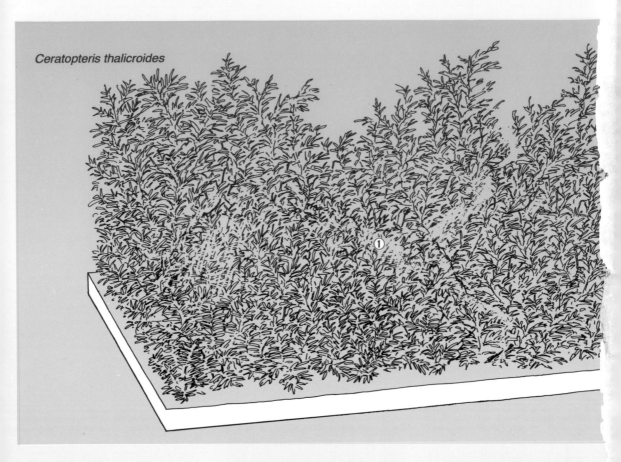

Ceratopteris thalicroides

**Above and Below:** *Poecilia reticulata*

artificial light will have to be intensified. Two or three 20-watt tubes are sufficient for an 80 cm (24 in.) aquarium. *Ceratopteris thalictroides* was selected for this brightly lit aquarium since it thrives under good light. In order to provide a filter bed for the undergravel filter, coarse sand needs to be spread over the filter plate. Undergravel filters are not very popular in aquariums with many plants as these type of filters seem to impede plant growth. If the plants lose color, fertilizer should be added directly to the aquarium water. It is advisable to use fast-acting, liquid fertilizer. Under optimal conditions the plants will grow noticeably and you can enjoy the luscious green of this underwater landscape.

You should be warned, however, that IMPROPER use of liquid fertilizer might result in a pea-soup green aquarium!

guppies prefer shallow water.

The substrate filter need not cover the entire bottom area; one-third of it is sufficient. Equally effective is a large capacity outside or power filter. In view of the color development of these fish and the required growth of the plants selected, the aquarium should be located at a site that is exposed to indirect natural daylight. Natural light has a substantial influence on the color of guppies. The metallic sheens in particular require natural light to be seen at their best. If there is no such location, the

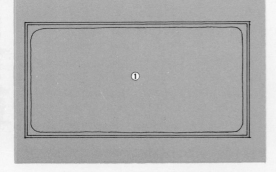

### SELECTING THE FISH

If this is a general guppy aquarium, one-third of the water should be changed once a week. It is essential to clean the bottom every four to eight weeks.

Since guppies are copious feeders, they should be given a diet of frozen foods and special guppy food available from most aquarium shops. The actual amount fed must be small, but there should be several feedings per day. This is particularly important when dealing with juvenile guppies; if these are not fed often enough the males will remain small and color development is poor. The diet has a strong influence on coloration. Females can become sterile or the number of their progeny will decline with an inadequate diet. In order to keep the basic guppy varieties within limits in an aquarium, it is best to initially buy only two to three pairs of high-quality

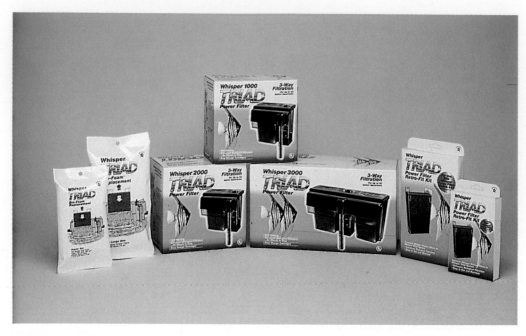

Outside power filters provide complete biological, chemical and mechanical filtration for use in the home aquarium. Photo courtesy of Tetra/Second Nature.

strains. Start out with those that are easy to breed true. Line-breeding particular guppy strains is something for specialists and it is very challenging. Guppies are often underestimated in this respect. Guppy breeding is exceedingly popular in Asia.

Simple breeding requires at least two aquariums; one for the parents and one for their progeny. The young born in the parent aquarium are transferred to the other tank about one week after they are born. Once they are about 2 cm (about 1 inch)

long, some of the young females may be returned to the parent aquarium. There they will cross-breed with their fathers. This method of back-crossing assures the body characteristics of particular strains over several generations. Those young that are not required for further breeding are kept together in the juvenile tank and disposed of to other hobbyists or sold to your local aquarium shop.

Guppies are among the most popular aquarium fishes. They still offer challenges and enjoyment even to professional aquarists.

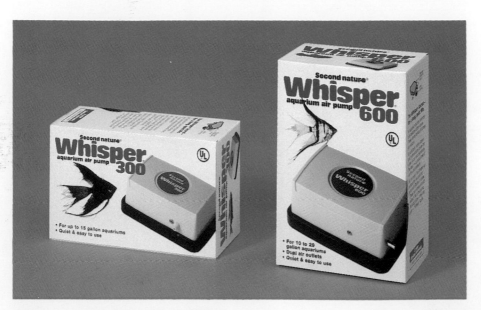

**Above:** Air pumps are necessary for the operation of many aquarium accessories including airstones, air-driven ornaments and air-driven filters. Make sure that the air pump you choose is powerful enough for the size aquarium you have and the specific accessory the pump is driving. Photo courtesy of Tetra/Second Nature.

**Right:** Fluorescent tubes for aquarium lighting fixtures come in a number of different wattages and light spectra—and of course some are much longer than others. Pet dealers can provide sensible advice about lighting choices. Photo courtesy of Penn Plax.

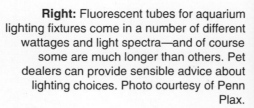

# CENTRAL & SOUTH AMERICA

DATA
*Water temperature:* 26° C (79°F).
*Tank dimensions:* 90 x 30 x 40 cm (36 x 12 x 16 in.)
all-glass tank.
*Lighting:* 2 x 30-watt bulbs.
*Daily illumination period:* 12 hours.
*Influx of daylight:* Sunlight through window.
*Substrate:* Coarse river sand.
*Filtration:* Power filter using a canister.
*Water changes:* ⅓ of total volume once every two
weeks.
*Heating:* 200-watt heater, thermostatically
controlled.
*Fertilizer:* Plant fertilizer mixed in with substrate.
Liquid fertilizer is added with each water change.
*Carbon dioxide:* Added via diffuser tube.
*Water quality:* pH 7.2. Total hardness, 4°DH.
*Carbon dioxide in solution:* 10 mg per liter.

*Cabomba australis* propagates freely. Just
plant a piece in the substrate and it will root
and grow.

Tetras are brilliantly colored little fishes that live quietly in the Amazon. These fish, which look like precious gems, are most effectively displayed in an aquarium decorated with plants from the Amazon River system. If the fish are in optimum condition they will display their best colors, and it is sheer enjoyment to watch them.

Beautiful fish require a suitably attractive backdrop. Tetras belong in an underwater landscape made up of South American water plants. Since the entire tank decoration is going to be based upon the attractive coloration of tetras, the plants must not be too overwhelming. Instead, emphasis must be placed on selecting and positioning pieces of driftwood.

In order to let plants appear as naturalistic as possible, one should not use too many different plant species. Rapidly growing stemmed plants should be established in the back of the tank. If the center of the tank is planted with tall plants, the colorful little tetras are no longer visible. Instead, their designated swimming space should be as large as possible. In order to recreate the mood of the Amazon, driftwood is of paramount importance. A blunt piece of wood is permitted to penetrate into the open water and all the way up to the surface so it looks as natural as possible. Tall plants are established

1 *Hydrocotyle leucopetala*  3 *Echinodorus bleheri*  5 *Alternanthera sessilis*  7 *Echinodorus quadricostatus*
2 *Cabomba australis*  4 *Mayaca vandelli*  6 *Echinodorus osiris*  8 *Heteranthera zosterifolia*

*Moenkhausia pittieri*

*Thoracocharax stellatus*

*Nannostomus marginatus*

*Hyphessobrycon scholzei*

*Aphyocharax rathbuni*

*Nematobrycon lacortei*

*Hyphessobrycon "robertsi"*

*Pristella maxillaris*

*Hemigrammus rodwayi*

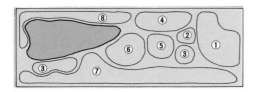

behind it and substrate-covering (creeping) plants in front of it. This provides sufficient swimming space for a number of different tetras. Tetras must always be kept in small schools to be esthetically impressive.

## SETTING UP THE TANK

The aquarium should be as long as possible; the longer the tank, the better the elegant schooling behavior of the fish can be seen. If tetra species, such as *Nematobrycon*, are being selected, the tank needs to be sufficiently large, since these fish form territories. Larger tanks are always more advantageous since they are easier to maintain. There are also advantages for the fish. Compared with specimens from small tanks, tetras (of the same species as in the small tank) that have been reared in large tanks reach a significantly larger maximum size.

As substrate we use coarse, dark river sand. Lighting must not be too strong. Two 30-watt lamps are sufficient for an aquarium that is 90 cm (36 in.) long. If the illumination is too strong, the fish will not display their best coloration.

Since tetras do not place a large bioload on the tank water, the filter does not need to be too powerful; a small power filter with a canister is quite sufficient.

## SELECTING THE PLANTS

For this specific South American tank we select water plants from the Amazon River. Stemmed plants are well-suited for such a particular habitat tank; however, because of the plant care required, the water will have to changed frequently.

Since stemmed plants generally grow fairly rapidly, they will soon fill up the swimming space of the fish. This must not be permitted since the esthetic emphasis is on the *movement* of these fast-swimming fish.

Consequently, rapidly growing plants are placed in the back of the aquarium. Those plants exhibiting slower growth are then placed in the center and the foreground of the aquarium. One very attractive plant in the center of the tank is *Alternanthera sessilis*, a slow-growing, stemmed plant.

To establish a contrast to the driftwood root, *Hydrocotyle leucocephala* has been planted on the right-hand side. This attractive water plant grows all the way to the surface. As far as trimming Amazon plants is concerned, only the dying leaves are cut off. *Heteranthera* and *Hydrocotyle* are trimmed only when they have reached the surface of the water and start bending over. In such an arrangement it is important that the foreground plants be only lightly pruned, since the plants in the back do not need that much light.

One-fourth to one-third of the entire water volume is changed every two weeks. Once the plants have ceased to thrive, carbon dioxide fertilization needs to be increased or plant fertilizer must be added.

## SELECTING THE FISHES

For a habitat display of this kind, colorful tetras are favored. Soft water with a small amount of acidity is just right. Once the fishes have adapted to

The male *Nannostomus marginatus* drives the egg-laden female through the *Cabomba* during spawning. The fertilized eggs are quickly eaten by the parents and other fishes in the aquarium unless some measures are taken for their protection.

this sort of water quality, they will display optimum coloration. Under ideal water conditions one particular attraction is *Nematobrycon* species. Normally this species has a reddish sheen along the sides. When kept in water of optimal quality, the dorsal, pelvic, and tail fins also turn red. *Hyphessobrycon "robertsi"* is equally responsive to water quality. Depending on the state of well-being of this fish, the viewer may get the impression that he is looking at different species. A specimen kept under optimal conditions will turn solid pink, but become increasingly paler as the water quality deteriorates. A similarly attractive fish is *Aphyocharax rathbuni*; its coloration can also be affected by water quality.

Another tetra which is always attractive is *Moenkhausia pittieri*. As a juvenile this species is fairly inconspicuous but adults develop a very beautiful metallic sheen.

**Above:** Many fish look and feel their best only when provided with tank conditions that are similar to the conditions in their native waters. A number of products useful in replicating the chemistry of native waters are available at pet shops. Photo courtesy of Aquarium Pharmaceuticals.

**Above:** *Moenkhausia pittieri* is commonly called the Diamond Tetra. The long violet-hued fins and highly iridescent scales make this active little beauty a major player in your Brazilian combo.
**Right:** *Hyphessobrycon robertsi*. This fish will let you know very quickly if your water quality is deteriorating. If they start to fade, check your water.

*Paracheirodon axelrodi,* the Cardinal Tetra, is considered to be the most beautiful small tropical fish in the world. It glows magnificently among green water plants. Its coloration—sometimes described as being "artificial," complements most suitably the conspicuous Ram Cichlid, *Microgeophagus ramirezi.* Both of these fishes display their principal color elements in red and blue, to which the Ram Cichlid also adds some yellow.

Since they are both small and peaceful, they are ideally suited to swim together among the water plants.

A narrow but long aquarium is best for bringing out the esthetics of a school of Cardinal Tetras. Among the schematically placed plants these fish will swim in a single file, while the entire school as such conveys the impression of being under variable illumination.

In contrast to the constantly moving *Paracheirodon, Microgeophagus* plays a much calmer role. Since this

Cardinal Tetras like the company of their fellows. A minimum of six Cardinals are required for the fish to exhibit their schooling behavior.

*Echinodorus quadricostatus* is an excellent foreground plant that will soon cover the bottom with its dense growth. Propagate by separating the young plants that form on long runners.

species remains relatively still, in terms of coloration it must be more conspicuous than *Paracheirodon axelrodi*. They pay little attention to the Cardinals while the Cardinals glide smoothly through the green aquascape.

Because both fishes are totally unrelated, their respective characteristics are even further enhanced. These fish came originally from South America, and so did the plants listed for this habitat display. The aquarium as such is long and low, and for that reason we use slow-growing stemmed plants. This also reduces the task of regular trimming. Here we are using principally *Echinodorus* species. In view of the height of the tank and the size of the fish, we use the miniature *Echinodorus quadricostatus* and *E. tenellus* as the main water plant species. In order to achieve some visual variety, to the left and to the right we plant *Alternanthera sessilis* and *Hydrocotyle leucocephala*. So that the back section does not appear barren, we place some fast-growing *Heteranthera zosteraefolia* there.

DATA
*Water temperature*: 25°C (77°F).
*Tank dimensions:* 125 x 35 x 40 cm acrylic tank.
*Lighting*: 3 x 20-watt lamps; 1 x 20-watt grow-light bulb.
*Daily illumination period:* 12 hours.
*Influx of daylight*: Gentle light up to midday.
*Substrate:* River sand.
*Filtration:* Canister filter.
*Water changes:* Up to ⅓ of tank volume every 10 days.
*Heating:* 150-watt heater.
*Fertilizer*: Mixed in with substrate.
*Water quality*: pH 7.2. Total hardness 4°DH.
*Carbon dioxide in solution*: 8 mg per liter.

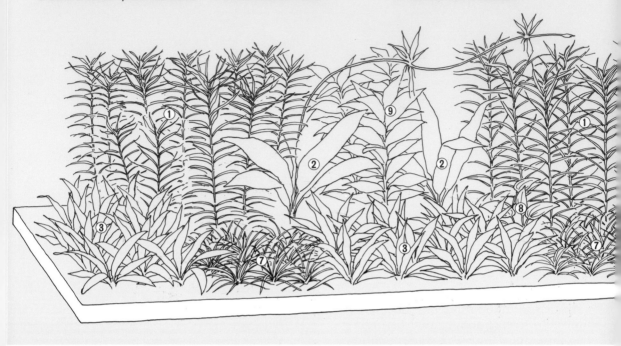

1 *Heteranthera zosteraefolia*  4 *Hydrocotyle leucocephala*  7 *Echinodorus tenellus*
2 *Echinodorus amazonicus*  5 *Echinodorus opacus*  8 *Echinodorus macrophyllus*
3 *Echinodorus quadricostatus*  6 *Echinodorus osiris*  9 *Alternanthera sessilis*

## SETTING UP THE TANK

A tetra tank should be long and narrow. In order to achieve successful root development of *Echinodorus quadricostatus*, it is advisable to have a substrate layer of river sand, at least 5 cm (2 in.) thick. Plant fertilizer can be mixed into the substrate, but it is better to "underdo it" than "overdo it," since the roots start to decay with excessive fertilization. For the same reason, the plants should not be immersed in the substrate deeper than 25 mm (1 in.). If they are placed too deep the small roots will not take hold properly. When planted shallower, the individual roots can find their own path. Filtration should be by means of a medium-sized canister filter. If there is spectacular plant growth, there are no problems. If, however, the plants do not seem to be growing, carbon dioxide fertilization must be increased.

## WATER PLANT CARE

If there is tremendous plant growth, plant care and maintenance are relatively pleasant and easy. The main plants, *Echinodorus quadricostatus*, do not require any trimming. If there are some runners that have become entangled, they can be simply cut off. *Alternanthera* should be shortened when the water surface has been reached. When *Heteranthera* reaches the surface, the long shoots are selectively cut off so that the young ones can catch up.

One-third of the water should be changed every 10 to 14 days. If the *Heteranthera, Hydrocotyle* and *Echinodorus quadricostatus* become discolored and turn white, a small amount of liquid fertilizer should be added. Apart from that, there should not be any carbon dioxide or liquid fertilizer supplements given to this tank. The number of fishes and fertilizer granulate mixed into the substrate will maintain the (chemical) equilibrium of the water.

## SELECTING THE FISHES

In spite of the number of aquarium fish species available, the Cardinal Tetra, *Paracheirodon axelrodi,* is still the leading beauty among small tropical fish. The Ram Cichlid is desirable because of its beauty and calm disposition. Since this fish can also coexist quite peacefully with other species, it is an ideal aquarium fish. This habitat aquarium is occupied by two South American fish families. The plants, too, are South American, although they do not grow side-by-side in the Amazon River. Yet, in an artificially constructed habitat such as the tank described here, these plants seem to get along quite well.

It is not an exaggeration to say that the intense coloration of the fishes and the luxuriant growth of the plants complement each other superbly well in this aquarium.

*Paracheirodon axelrodi*
*Microgeophagus ramirezi*

A school of Cardinal Tetras.

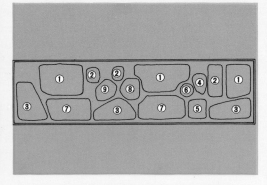

This is an attempt to set up a South American water landscape of the Amazon River. It is, of course, impossible to depict all characteristics of the Amazon River in a single aquarium. Although "Amazonas" is only a simple, single word, it covers an incredibly large and diverse aquatic environment. Still, it is entertaining for the home aquarist to attempt to reconstruct at least a small segment of this very interesting region. Many of its smaller tributaries, where a similar scene could conceivably exist, are fed by small creeks. In this case, it is a typical scene where *Corydoras* form small "troops" and where *Hyphessobrycon* playfully move among the water plants. This scene is, of course, thousands of miles away from the Amazon River and here there are no massive mud floods churning up the water. Instead, our fishes enjoy crystal-clear water. In fact, all we are doing here is creating a scene that could be reminiscent of the Amazon River because the reality cannot be duplicated in an aquarium situation.

*Echinodorus* swordplants are bathed in bright tropical sunlight so there is strong leaf growth. Nature can not be duplicated, yet this tank is set up in such a way that a natural atmosphere occurs. Basically, for this aquarium we use a lot of driftwood and *Echinodorus amazonicus*

# SWORDPLANTS

DATA
*Water temperature*: 25°C (77°F).
*Tank dimensions*: 100 x 45 x 45 cm (40 x 18 x 18 in.)all-glass tank.
*Lighting*: 2 x 30-watt bulb.
*Daily illumination:* 15 hours.
*Influx of daylight:* None.
*Substrate:* River sand.
*Filtration:* Outside filter with three chambers.
*Water changes*: ⅓ of tank volume once per 14 days.
*Heating*: 200-watt heater, thermostatically-controlled.
*Fertilization:* Fertilizer mixed in with substrate.
Carbon dioxide added via diffuser pipe.
*Water quality:* pH 7.0.
*Total hardness:* 5°DH.
*Carbon dioxide in solution:* 10 mg per liter.

*Hemiodopsis semitaeniatus* are built for speed and jumping. Cover your tank well and don't keep them with easily frightened tankmates.

*Corydoras agassizii*

*Hyphessobrycon callistus callistus*

*Aequidens metae*

*Corydoras leopardus*

*Hemiodopsis semitaeniatus*

*Apistogramma steindachneri*

*Dianema urostriatum*

*Nannostomus harrisoni*

*Aequidens curviceps*

1 *Echinodorus osiris*
2 *Echinodorus amazonicus*
3 *Echinodorus horizontalis*
4 *Limnobium laevigatum*
5 *Hydrocotyle leucocephala*

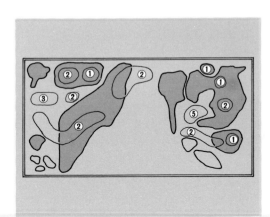

## SETTING UP THE TANK

Since this aquarium is to depict the Amazon River, we have to select a very large tank. As bottom substrate we must use river sand. To simulate exposed tree roots from the river banks, we select a number of differently formed pieces of driftwood root stocks. These are to form the very foundation of this habitat tank.

Since the *Echinodorus* are to grow (epiphytically) on these driftwood pieces, we cut out the required holes and depressions with a carving knife. In order to simulate a river bed we place the driftwood pieces in a step-like arrangement. It does not matter if some of the river sand flows out of the cracks between adjacent pieces of wood; quite to the contrary, the slightly wavy sand deposits which have accumulated in this manner give the entire scene an even more natural appearance. The tank illumination should be slightly more subdued than for tanks with stemmed plants. The lights are focused directly above the planted sections of the tank. As the plant nucleus we select healthy *Echinodorus* species. They are buried in the holes and crevasses dug into roots and other driftwood pieces or are planted directly behind the step-like arrangement of driftwood toward the back of the tank.

As fertilizer, we can use quality plant fertilizer, and using forceps, bury individual grains or pellets into the substrate in the planted tank sections. These pellets should be placed in the substrate about 3 to 4 cm away from the plants so that the roots do not come into direct contact with the fertilizer. For filtration we use an outside filter or a power filter with a canister. If the tank is heavily populated with fishes, a suitably powerful (high-capacity) filter must be installed.

becomes the dominant type of plant. In order to achieve the atmosphere of a river bottom, the foreground of the tank does not contain any plants and is only covered with river sand. *Limnobium laevigatum* are drifting on the surface. This creates shade below the surface and provides adequate cover for the fishes below. Moreover, the long thread-like roots offer excellent hiding places for juvenile fish.

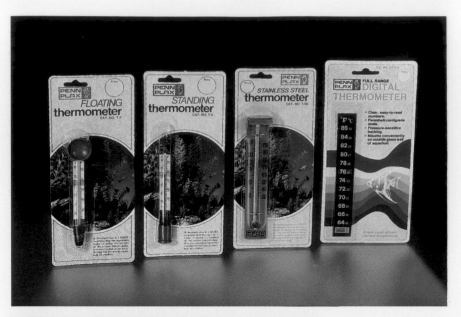

Above: There are many types of thermometers to determine the temperature of your aquarium water, including floating, standing, hanging and digital. Photo courtesy of Penn Plax.

**Left:** *Hyphessobrycon callistus* is a peaceful little tetra that likes plenty of plants and a dark background on the tank.

## SELECTING THE FISHES

To convey an Amazon-like atmosphere we select medium-sized fish. As a true representative of the Amazon River and as the dominant species we select the intensely colored *Hyphessobrycon callistus* even though no Amazonian tank is complete without the Cardinal Tetra, *Paracheirodon axelrodi*, which actually comes from the Rio Negro and not the Amazon. *Corydoras* and *Loricaria* are most suitable as bottom dwellers. We should not forget *Aequidens curviceps,* another representative of the South American fish fauna. *Aequidens metae* is a medium-sized fish and most suitable for the overall tank concept under discussion. From the genus *Apistogramma*, we select a small species, such as *Apistogramma steindachneri*, which tends to remain as inconspicuously as possible in the *Echinodorus* forest.

If, as we have done for the plants, we select fishes that are similarly robust, maintaining a habitat aquarium like this is very simple and the enjoyment of such a tank can last for a long time.

Top quality 6-month-old blue guppies.

This habitat aquarium is created by using fishes and plants from North and Central America. Selected from among the group of livebearers we have *Xiphophorus* and *Poecilia* with their tall dorsal fins, swimming among luxuriously growing water plants. In fact, principally green water plants have been selected so that the conspicuousness of the fishes is even further emphasized. All plant and fish species used here come from North or Central America.

Just as we have done with stemmed plants, all plant groups here are planted at the same time. The aesthetic diversity is created through variable heights of plants in the back, the center, and in the foreground of the tank. Such a

DATA
*Water temperature*: 22 °C (72°F).
*Tank dimensions*: 80 x 50 x 40 cm acrylic tank.
*Lighting*: 3 x 20-watt bulbs.
*Daily illumination*: 12 hours.
*Influx of daylight*: None.
*Substrate*: Coarse river sand.
*Filtration*: Rapid filter.
*Water changes*: ⅓ of tank volume once a week.
*Heating*: Ambient (room) temperature; possible supplementation by thermostatically controlled heater.
*Fertilizer*: Plant fertilizer mixed in with substrate; liquid fertilizer added during water changes.
*Carbon dioxide*: Given via diffuser pipe.
*Water quality*: pH 7.0.
*Total hardness*: 5° DH
*Carbon dioxide in solution*: 12 mg per liter.

The intensely colorful platies provide a lovely contrast with the fresh green of the plants.

planting arrangement also creates a comfortable environment for the fishes. Because of the exclusive use of green plants, the overall appearance of the tank is calming and the glorious colors of the fishes become the focal point of attention.

The plants listed prefer low water temperatures and shallow water. For this reason they do not go well with *Poecilia velifera*, which need a high temperature. The plants can, however, be gradually acclimated to an intermediate temperature that is suitable for both fishes and plants. *Xiphophorus* can be kept at a lower temperature without any problems.

The rapidly growing plants supply the fishes continuously with new oxygen so that they appear noticeably content in this green forest.

### SETTING UP THE TANK

A tank 80 to 100 cm (32-40 in.) long is quite suitable for the active *Poecilia*. The substrate should consist of coarse river sand with plant fertilizer mixed in. North American water plants are different than those from Southeast Asia and Africa. They grow in rural areas and are accustomed to lots of sunlight. Therefore, rearing them in an aquarium requires lower water temperatures than we would maintain for an Amazonian tank. An adequate supply of carbon dioxide and strong illumination may be necessary.

For an 80 cm (32 in.) long tank we therefore use two to three bulbs of 20 watts each, and for a 100 cm (40 in.)long aquarium it is advisable to use three to four bulbs at 20 watts each. Only fluorescent tubes which emit a warm light should be installed. These tubes not only enhance the green color of the plants, but at the same time they lend a natural appearance to the red coloration in fishes.

## SELECTING THE WATER PLANTS

We select plants which principally have their origin in North America, such as *Ludwigia repens x palustris, Didiplis diandra, Hemianthus micranthemoides, Lobelia cardinalis,* and *Sagittaria. Echinodorus berteroi, Gymnocoronis spilanthoides, Cabomba piauhyensis, Hydrocotyle verticillata* and *Echinodorus tenellus,* which are found in Mexico and South America, can also be used.

Nearly all water plants prefer low water temperatures. During the summer the relationship between light and temperature is large. The water must be changed frequently and the maximum temperature must not exceed 28°C (82°F). During the winter, however, temperatures around 21 to 22°C (70°F) are sufficient. During periods of lower temperature the plants require less light, which in turn means that fewer water changes are required.

Since plants grow slower at lower water temperatures, trimming them becomes an easy task. *Cabomba piauhyensis* does not grow well if there is insufficient dissolved carbon dioxide in the water. On the other hand, *Ludwigia* and *Didiplis,* which prefer hard water, are bound to grow very well.

The rapidly growing *Gymnocoronis spilanthoides* in the back of the tank needs to be trimmed frequently so that they do not reach the water surface. The slow-growing *Didiplis diandra* and *Ludwigia* rarely need to be shortened. Moreover, they do not like to be transplanted.

## SELECTING THE FISHES

*Poecilia* and *Xiphophorus* like slightly saline water; however, since plants cannot tolerate water with a high salt content, salt must NOT be added to the tank once it has been completely set up. If livebearers are transferred from water that contains some salt into pure fresh water, there is a possibility that this change in water condition can cause the outbreak of diseases. Therefore, it is advisable that such fishes be acclimated gradually to the new water conditions in a separate tank before they are transferred into this newly set up tank. Once the fishes have adjusted to salt-free water they can then be transferred to the newly set up aquarium. When buying fish you should also ascertain whether the fish have been kept in water to which salt has been added. If this was not the case, acclimatization is not necessary.

Dr. Herbert R. Axelrod uses the Lakes Malawi-Tanganyika salts made by Dr. Biener and sold in pet shops that specialize in cichlids. He adds the dosage recommended for cichlids, and reduces it slowly over a period of

Plugs provide a rooting medium and also provide fertilizer for living plants. Photo courtesy of Aquarium Products.

1 *Shinnersia rivulatus*
2 *Ludwigia arcuata*
3 *Echinodorus parviflorus*
4 *Sagittaria graminea*
5 *Echinodorus tenellus*
6 *Lobelia cardinalis*
7 *Hydrocotyle verticillata*
8 *Cabomba piauhyensis*
9 *Myriophyllum hippuroides*

10 *Bacopa caroliniana*
11 *Hemianthus micranthemoides*
12 *Gymnocornis spilanthoides*
13 *Didiplis diandra*
14 *Echinodorus berteroi*
15 *Ludwigia repens*
16 *Sagittaria subulata*

*Poecilia velifera*
*Xiphophorus maculatus*

*Xiphophorus maculatus*
*Xiphophorus maculatus*

*Xiphophorus helleri*
*Xiphophorus maculatus*

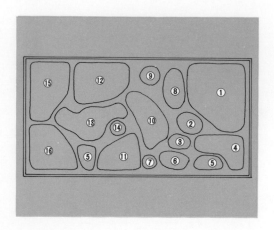

made of 100% vegetable matter. Read the label carefully, as many so-called "vegetable" foods contain fillers that are not of vegetable origin. One of the consequences of heavy food consumption by fish is the accumulation of waste products that place a severe biological load on the water. Therefore, if a large number of fishes are kept in this tank and they are properly fed, it is essential to provide strong filtration. In addition, regular partial water changes will also improve the overall water quality.

The mode of reproduction in livebearers is interesting. As already indicated by their common name, female livebearers give birth to fully developed, live young. Since the parents, however, have strong cannibalistic tendencies towards their own young, it is advisable to set up a special rearing tank for the young. This way the can be protected from their own parents for the first few weeks of their life, and until they have reached sub-adulthood.

72 hours.

Livebearers develop a strong appetite and will eat a lot. In addition to live foods, they also require some vegetable matter in their diet. This can be supplemented with fish foods

Albino Lyretail Molly

Lyretail Molly

Black Molly

Sailfin Molly

A handsome pair of Swordtails. There are many strains available for the interested hobbyist.

The beautiful marbled Sailfin Molly will add beauty and interest to any community of livebearers.

DATA
*Water temperature:* 26°C (80°F).
*Tank dimensions:* 80 x 80 x 30 cm (32 x 32 x 12 in.) acrylic tank.
*Lighting:* 4 x 20-watt fluorescent tubes.
*Illumination period:* 12 hours.
*Influx of daylight:* None.
*Substrate:* River sand.
*Filtration:* Outside filter with canister.
*Water changes:* ⅓ of tank volume once a week.
*Heating:* 150-watt heater, thermostatically controlled.
*Fertilizer:* Soil fertilizer added to substrate. Addition of liquid fertilizer during water change is recommended. Carbon dioxide supplementation via diffuser pipe is also recommended.
*Water quality:* pH 6.9.
*Carbonate hardness:* 30° DH
*Carbon dioxide in solution:* 8 mg per liter.

The "lawn" of *Echinodorus quadricostatus* will need to be "mowed" occasionally. Without some trimming, the plants will soon fill the viewing area.

Among the river systems of the Amazon and Paraguay Rivers, there are so-called "cristalinos." To the same degree that there are mud floods in the Amazon River, there are also waterways where the water is clear and transparent. Invariably the bottom of these rivers is densely covered with algae and water plants and gives the appearance of a green carpet, reflecting bright sunlight. If one approaches the river bank, schools of small fish will dart into deeper water. To find out what species these fish are, one has to approach very quietly. Usually these fish are small catfishes of the large genus *Corydoras*. They live in small schools in shallow areas of the clear-water rivers and streams.

It is exactly this scene that we are trying to duplicate in this natural aquarium. Even though this is a tank for *Corydoras*, its proper layout and assembly is quite difficult. In a densely planted tank, these fish will not be visible. On the other hand, if we omit plants altogether it would be a boring display.

*Corydoras* swim along the bottom

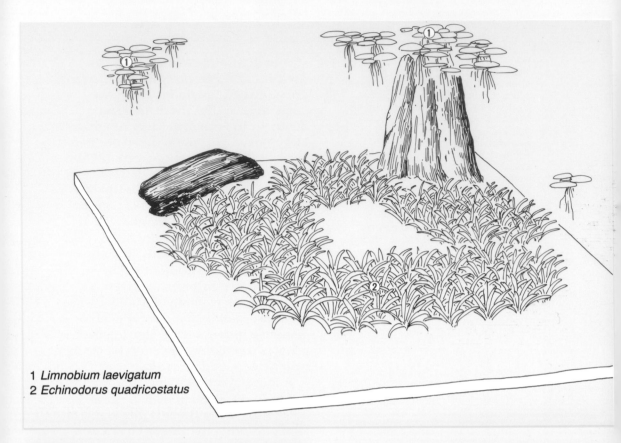

1 *Limnobium laevigatum*
2 *Echinodorus quadricostatus*

*Mesonauta festivus*

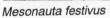
Shrimp

*Corydoras* sp.

*Corydoras schwartzi*

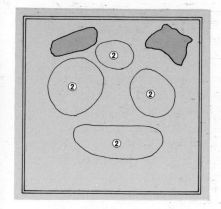

and over plants that grow along shallow river and stream banks. The *Corydoras* stay in small groups above the plants and sometimes they swim down to the barren substrate, resting there or looking for food.

A totally naturalistic underwater scene is rare in an aquarium. In order to bring a bit of diversity into the tank, driftwood is placed in the back to provide hiding places for the *Corydoras*. This also reduces stress in a tank that has a limited height. It is not only supposed to be a breeding tank but at the same time an attractive habitat aquarium.

Looking down into the tank and watching the highly active *Corydoras* moving about is a tremendous viewing pleasure. This is indeed a very special and highly fascinating aquarium.

## SETTING UP THE TANK

The tank depicted in the illustration is 80 x 80 x 30 cm (32 x 32 x 12 in.). The area is large but the height is low. In order to breed *Corydoras* it is important to use a tank with a large (bottom) area.

Another important factor is the substrate when breeding *Corydoras*. Since they tend to dig through the sand in search of food it is imperative to use very small-grained sand. For optimum plant growth the fertilizer gets mixed into the substrate. The

It is unusual to look down on cichlids in an aquarium, but this arrangement gives one the feeling of gazing into a koi pond.

plants must not be planted too closely to each other. When breeding *Corydoras*, which always have a healthy appetite, it best to use a large capacity external (power) filter. Such a filter creates a strong water current, which tends to increase the activities of *Corydoras* even further. At the same time, the current stimulates these small catfishes to spawn. A prerequisite is a nutritious diet. Natural light is best if we want to achieve a genuine atmosphere in this tank. *Corydoras* swim to the surface in order to take in atmospheric oxygen (air), and so cause circular water ripples that set off a rippling light effect through the tank. If the tank is positioned so that we cannot take advantage of natural lighting, the planted areas of the tank must then be exposed to fluorescent illumination. Twenty-watt fluorescent tubes should be installed, the number of which are determined by the size of the tank.

## SELECTING THE FISHES

"Cristalinos" are inhabited by various fish species. Here we are only dealing with a specific habitat tank that depicts a scene typical of a river bank. The yellow-bellied cichlid females are busy protecting their young; close by are schools of *Corydoras*. These *Corydoras* are suitable for this tank; however, since their coloration is very similar to that of the bottom, they are very inconspicuous and it is difficult to focus the viewer's attention on them.

The dominant species to select is *Corydoras schwartzi*, which is conspicuous in coloration and pattern. They are clearly distinguishable from all the other *Corydoras*, and moreover they are very attractive. For supporting roles we can select other *Corydoras* species. In order to bring some action into this picture we then select *Mesonauta festivus*. This cichlid species is active but peaceful and establishes territories.

In order to achieve a genuine "mood" reminiscent of being close to a river bank, it is better to introduce juvenile specimens than adult fish into this natural habitat aquarium.

The Flag Cichlid (*Mesonauta festivus*) is graced with good looks and a nice personality.

The Peppered Cory (*Corydoras paleatus*) is very popular and easy to find in almost any shop that sells tropical fishes.

# SOUTHEAST ASIA

Here we are dealing with an aquarium where there is luxuriant growth of *Microsorium pteropus*. This could be described as a very natural aquarium. This plant species occurs over wide areas of Southeast Asia and India. It appears as wild grass in tropical rain forests, along mountain streams and waterfalls. It always grows in abundance in areas exposed to water sprays. In tropical regions, the leaves of this plant remain above the water level during the dry season; during the rainy season they become totally immersed below water. There are even a few locations in highly developed Japan and the Pine Barrens of New Jersey where this plant still occurs.

In a large tank these deep-green water plants should always be planted closely together. Swimming in this plant forest we find attractively colored barbs, which also originated in Southeast Asia. A magical and tasteful picture—as can be found in Southeast Asia—has been created by using only these two components, fishes and plants.

*Microsorium pteropus* belongs to the healthiest and hardiest of water plants. Their roots can establish themselves in gravel substrate, on rocks as well as on driftwood. The plants as such, the leaves, the rhizome, and the roots are extraordinarily strong and durable. This plant does best in a sandy substrate and at a water temperature of 22°C (72°F).

A number of flat rocks form the foundation for this habitat tank. They are stacked on top of each other, and the roots of the plants are inserted into the interspace between adjacent rocks. In those spots where it is difficult to secure plants we use a black cotton or

DATA:
Water temperature: 24°C (75°F).
Tank dimensions: 120 x 45 x 45 cm (48 x 18 x 18 in.) all-glass tank.
Lighting: 2 x 20-watt lamps.
Daily illumination period: up to 16 hours.
Influx of daylight: Soft natural light up to midday.
Substrate: Coarse river sand.
Filtration: External filter with canister.
Water changes: ⅓ of total tank volume every 2 weeks.
Heating: 200-watt thermostatically-controlled heater.
Fertilizer: None.
Water quality: pH 6.8.
Total hardness: 3° DH.
Carbon dioxide in solution: 8 mg per liter.

**Left**: Java fern is one of the most hardy aquatic plants.
**Right:** If you have difficulty with aquatic plants, Java fern is likely to grow well for you.
**Below:** Rasboras are found in the same waters as the Java fern.

*Rasbora hengeli*
*Rasbora vaterifloris*

*Chela dadyburjori*
*Rasbora agilis*

*Rasbora einthoveni*
*Rasbora heteromorpha*

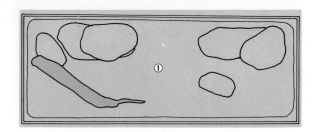

1 *Microsorium pteropus*

filtration devices that create a strong water current. The illumination does not need to be particularly strong. A 20 watt lamp is sufficient for 60 cm (24 in.)long tank, or two lamps for a 90 cm (36 in.) long tank. The plants will grow according to the picture shown here, and in the process will develop interesting leaf shapes. When the lighting is deployed mainly over the foreground of the tank we will see pretty leaf shapes and luxuriant growth. The illumination should be provided by means of growth-enhancing fluorescent tubes, which also emphasize the green of *Microsorium* much more prominently.

## PLANT CARE

*Microsorium pteropus* belongs to the lowest form of ferns. Apart from a tiny amount of potassium they do require a lot of ammonia as fertilizer. For that reason the number of fish, as ammonia producers, should be high. Normally the water needs to be changed frequently in densely planted tanks. Yet, in a display featuring *Microsorium pteropus* it is sufficient to change a third of the volume only every two to three weeks. A peculiar plant disease affecting aquatic ferns often breaks out during late summer and during periods of high water temperatures. If plant growth is dense, losses among the plants will be correspondingly high. Diseased and dying leaves are removed (cut out). Affected runners are carefully identified and they must then also be removed. Moreover, it is important to

silk thread to attach the roots to enable them to become established. If this procedure is followed closely, the roots will grow onto the rocks and the driftwood within two to four weeks and soon thereafter new runners will develop. The foreground of the tank is covered with new runners of *Microsorium pteropus*. Here the roots were simply pushed into the sand; the rhizome as such must never be buried. As soon as the runners in the foreground have properly developed and start to grow they are then transplanted to the back of the tank. This way the overall plant density increases gradually. *Microsorium* grows slowly, but its hardiness and durability is unsurpassed by other water plants.

## SETTING UP THE TANK

Java fern as well as barbs prefer oxygen-rich water. For that reason coarse sand is the best choice for the bottom substrate. Java fern also likes water currents; therefore, we use make sure that during the summertime the temperature in the breeding tank is not too high. It is advisable to take precautions that the water temperature does not exceed 28°C (82°F). The illumination, for instance, produces a lot of heat. This can be taken into consideration when selecting the rod heater. Aquariums with a cover should be opened up during periods of high ambient temperatures, so that heat accumulating over the water surface can escape.

## SELECTING THE FISHES

Rasbora should become the focal point of attention in this tank. These small fish, from Southeast Asia are very popular. They do not nibble on the plants and they are also very attractively colored. We select small species, such as *Rasbora maculata, Rasbora heteromorpha, Rasbora hengeli* and *Rasbora agilis.* If possible, these fish should be introduced more or less at the same time. It is not advisable to keep adding fish, because this increases the risk of introducing diseases into the aquarium. In any event, all newly purchased fish should undergo a mandatory quarantine period in a separate tank.

Generally, barbs are peaceful, schooling fish that are always active. When they are being well fed, some may even spawn among the densely-growing plants; however, all Rasbora have a tendency to eat their own eggs, so that they can really only be bred successfully in a separate breeding tank.

The jewel tones of a school of *Rasbora heteromorpha* are beautifully set off by the Java ferns.

**Above left:** *Cryptocoryne walkeri* is one of the hardiest of the *Cryptocoryne* species. **Above right:** Terrestrial plants are an important part of this jungle aquarium.

DATA:
*Water temperature*: 23°C (72.5°F).
*Tank dimensions*: 90 x 45 x 45 cm (36 x 18 x 18 in.) all-glass tank.
*Lighting*: 5 x 30-watt fluorescent tubes or 2 x HQL lamps.
*Period of illumination*: 12 hours daily.
*Influx of daylight*: Soft light during the afternoon.
*Substrate*: Coarse river sand.
*Filtration*: Filter canister with power head and spray bar.
*Water changes*: Up to one-third of tank volume once a week.
*Heating*: 150-watt heater, thermostatically controlled or canister filter with built-in heater, e.g. Type EHEIM.
*Fertilizer*: Soil fertilizer mixed in with substrate, addition of liquid fertilizer during water change.
*Carbon dioxide*: Addition via diffuser pipe.
*Water quality*: pH 6.9.
*Total hardness*: 4°DH.
*Carbon dioxide in solution:* 6 mg/liter.

The tropical rivers of Southeast Asia are the home of Cryptocorynes. In this natural habitat aquarium we are trying to imitate the areas these plants occur in the wild. There are hardly any aquariums around where Cryptocorynes grow so densely that they cover the entire bottom to create a picture as we can see it in the wild. This creation is an attempt to depict a cross-section of the native Cryptocoryne's habitat. Considering the water depth at which these plants normally occur, the water in this tank is relatively shallow. All plants are actually planted in the water-covered areas. It is characteristic to see Cryptocorynes growing everywhere along the bottom of small streams.

Close to the stream banks are ferns that have grown from among the roots of trees, and various grasses which have not (yet) been identified. Up the river bank this is closely followed by dense jungle. But there is also something moving in the water! If we approach cautiously and look closely into the water we see intensely red *Puntius titteya*, which dart among the Cryptocorynes.

### SETTING UP THE TANK

A tank with the dimensions of 90 x 45 x 45 cm (36 x 18 x 18 in.) was chosen for this display. In view of the speed with which these plants grow, pushing their leaves partially above the surface, a suitably tall tank must

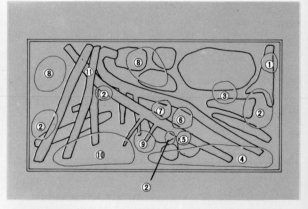

*Puntius titteya*
*Garra* sp.

*Puntius oligolepis*

be selected. In order to maintain the required humidity, such a display aquarium must always be properly covered. Cryptocorynes that normally grow submerged do not have the capacity to stabilize to their surroundings. Fertilization of the substrate is important in order to avoid any die-off among newly planted Cryptocorynes. In terrariums, where large parts are not submerged, a lot of light is lost. The terrestrial plants create a lot of shade. For that reason, artificial lighting, such as mercury vapor lamps, should be deployed. If possible, natural daylight should also be utilized.

River sand is used as bottom substrate. The rocks, which create the foundation of this display, are placed along the back of the tank. There they are combined with tube-shaped driftwood. Water depth is only 15 cm (6 in.).

## SELECTING THE PLANTS

In order to establish the foundation of the display, the terrestrial plants are introduced first. These include the genera *Aglaonema* and *Lagenandora*. Their roots are planted in the submerged bottom substrate, but their leaves protrude above the surface.

## COMMON LEAF PLANTS:

If the roots of *Chamedorea elegans* and those of *Ficus* become submerged they will die;

consequently, they will have to be planted above the water line. Moss grows on driftwood above the water line; *Fontinalis antipyretica* is one of the simple mosses. Moss must be kept moist until it has become firmly established. It is often visually very effective to create artificial "rain," using the filter discharge as a spray bar.

Plants such as *Aglaonema* stabilize their surroundings, since they will absorb excessive fertilizer. From among the Cryptocorynes we select small-leaved forms such as *C. beckettii* and *C. walkeri*. It is better to use a large number of specimens of the same species than many different species. Since Cryptocorynes are rather sensitive to changes in water quality it is possible that they will not grow properly. Water changes should only be made after all water plants have become firmly established. Once the functions of the tank have become stabilized, one-quarter to one-third of the entire water volume should be changed regularly every week.

## SELECTING THE FISHES

Barbs are ideal for capturing the atmosphere of Southeast Asia habitats. *Puntius titteya* is very common in these areas. This is a small, very beautiful fish that is quite peaceful. Moreover, it can be easily kept in a terrarium with small water areas.

Other recommended fish species are *Capoeta oligolepis* and *Rasbora heteromorpha*. These two species also occur frequently in those areas where Cryptocorynes are growing. If an aquarium is to appear natural, it is better to select a number of specimens of the same species, rather than of different species. Adherence to this principle is particularly important for those aquariums with a relatively small water volume.

77

DATA
*Water temperature.* 25°C (77°F)
Tank dimensions: 80 x 30 x 35 cm
all-glass tank
*Lighting:* 2 x 20-watt lamps.
*Daily illumination period.* 12 hours.
*Influx of daylight:* None
*Substrate:* Coarse river sand.
*Filtration:* Inside filter with filter chamber.
*Water changes:* ¼ of tank volume once a week.
*Heating:* 100-watt heater thermostatically-controlled.
*Fertilizer.* Fertilizer mixed in with substrate,
supplemented by addition of liquid fertilizer with
water changes
*Carbon dioxide:* supplement via diffuser pipe
*Water quality:* pH 6.9
*Total hardness.* 3° DH
*Carbon dioxide in solution* 8 mg per liter.

This is our suggestion for a display for people who are setting up an aquarium with water plants for the first time and for people who do not have much self-confidence when it comes to rearing and caring for water plants. The plants that are going to be used are those belonging to the genus of healthy and cheap *Hygrophila*. These water plants, which originated in India, are considered to be particularly hardy and because of their low price they are also very popular.

After breeding tropical fish became popular, water plants, most notably the *Hygrophila* species as used here, became well known and they are still very popular to this day. There are approximately 30 *Hygrophila* species world-wide. Nearly all them develop very attractive leaves under water. Moreover, as aquarium plants they are easy to grow. Green is the basic

*H. angustifolia* is its long and narrow leaves, etc. With help from the variable *Hygrophila* species it is easy to set up an attractive aquarium. In many tanks, where a lot of reddish plants have been used, it is the *Hygrophila* which convey an impression of being fresh and alive.

## SETTING UP THE TANK

For this aquarium we use a standard 80 cm (32 in.) tank. The bottom substrate consists of coarse sand. An inside filter is totally adequate here. But this is not enough to assure adequate plant growth. Fertilizer will have to be mixed into the substrate. Using a pair of planting tongs, we place one to two large pellets of plant fertilizer at 5 cm (2 in.) intervals into the substrate. If

Danios and White Clouds cavort among the leaves of the *Hygrophila*.

coloration of water plants; however, within the green spectrum *Hygrophila* has the most attractive and the most gentle greens. Especially, the green of the prolific and spreading *H. polisperma* is extraordinarily beautiful. This plant is found in many aquariums.

Since all members of this genus have the same general color tone, there are people who believe that a tank planted exclusively with these species can easily appear monotonous. But here too, each plant is an individual exhibit element. Each species is highly variable in leaf shape and over-all shape. *Hygrophila polysperma* has the basic form of a water plant, while *H. corymbosa* has stemmed leaves. A characteristic of

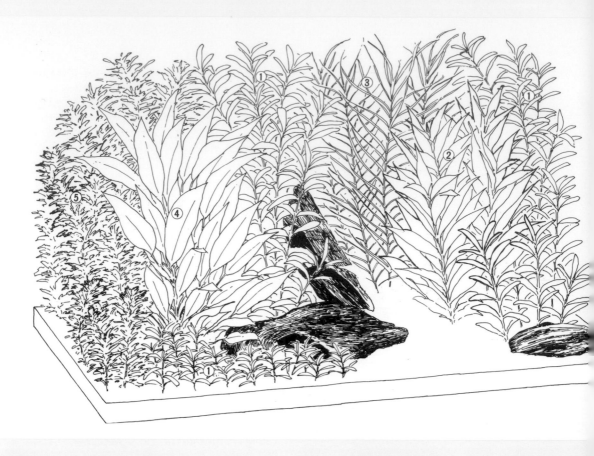

*Brachydanio rerio*
*Tanichthys albonubes* variety

*Tanichthys albonubes*
*Brachydanio frankei* variety

**Facing page:**
1 *Hygrophila polysperma*
2 *Hygrophila stricta*
3 *Hygrophila angustifolia*
4 *Hygrophila corymbosa*
5 *Hygrophila difformis*

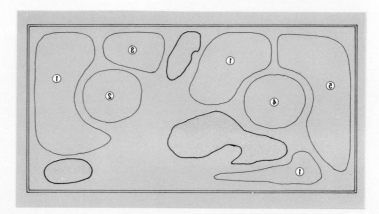

soil fertilizer is not used, liquid fertilizer will have to be added to the water. *Hygrophila* needs a lot of light for good growth. If the tank is located where there is access to daylight, this should be taken advantage of. Should there be no natural light available, artificial lighting by means of two 20-watt bulbs for an 80 cm aquarium must be provided. White fluorescent light gives *Hygrophila* a white, sickish appearance. Special growth-enhancing fluorescent lights not only emphasize the gentle green of these plants, but also facilitate their proper growth.

## SELECTING THE PLANTS

The first to be planted are the *H. polysperma.* When planted in an aquarium, new leaves will develop quickly under water. If the leaves become discolored and are turning white, the reason is either a lack of potassium or poor water quality. Even with weekly water changes, these plants initially tend to age quicker due to the substrate. Should this happen, a third of the water volume should be replaced daily over three successive days, and a small amount of liquid fertilizer should be added. Thereafter, we return to regular weekly water changes, together with a little bit of fertilizer. An incorrect light volume and wrong fertilizer will manifest themselves in the shapes of the leaves.

*Hygrophila stricta* and *H. corymbosa* need more light and a more fertile substrate than other *Hygrophila* species. If they do not get enough light, the lower leaves will drop off. Without adequate fertilizer the leaves (except the veins) will turn yellow. On the other hand, *H. angustifolia* develops very well under standard conditions. Moreover, this species does not get particularly large and is relatively hardy. If, however, it does not get enough light, it too will lose its lower leaves.

## SELECTING THE FISHES

The fish for this tank also originate in Southeast Asia. Any aquarist who has ever bred Zebra Danios, will keep them again. They are extremely hardy and can easily adapt to variable water conditions. They can even tolerate slight temperature variations without getting sick. There are many other delightful "danios." *Brachydanio rerio* is particularly attractive, as well as *B. frankei*, which moves its long fins like a butterfly, or the pretty pearl-colored *B. albolineatus*. Apart from the danios, we must not forget *Tanichthys albonubes*, the White Cloud Mountain Minnow that comes from China. As long as this fish is small it is largely blue, but as the fish grows it turns more and more red. This is a fish which is not only healthy and hardy, but one which displays interesting schooling behavior.

# 15
# WATER LILIES IN INDOOR PONDS

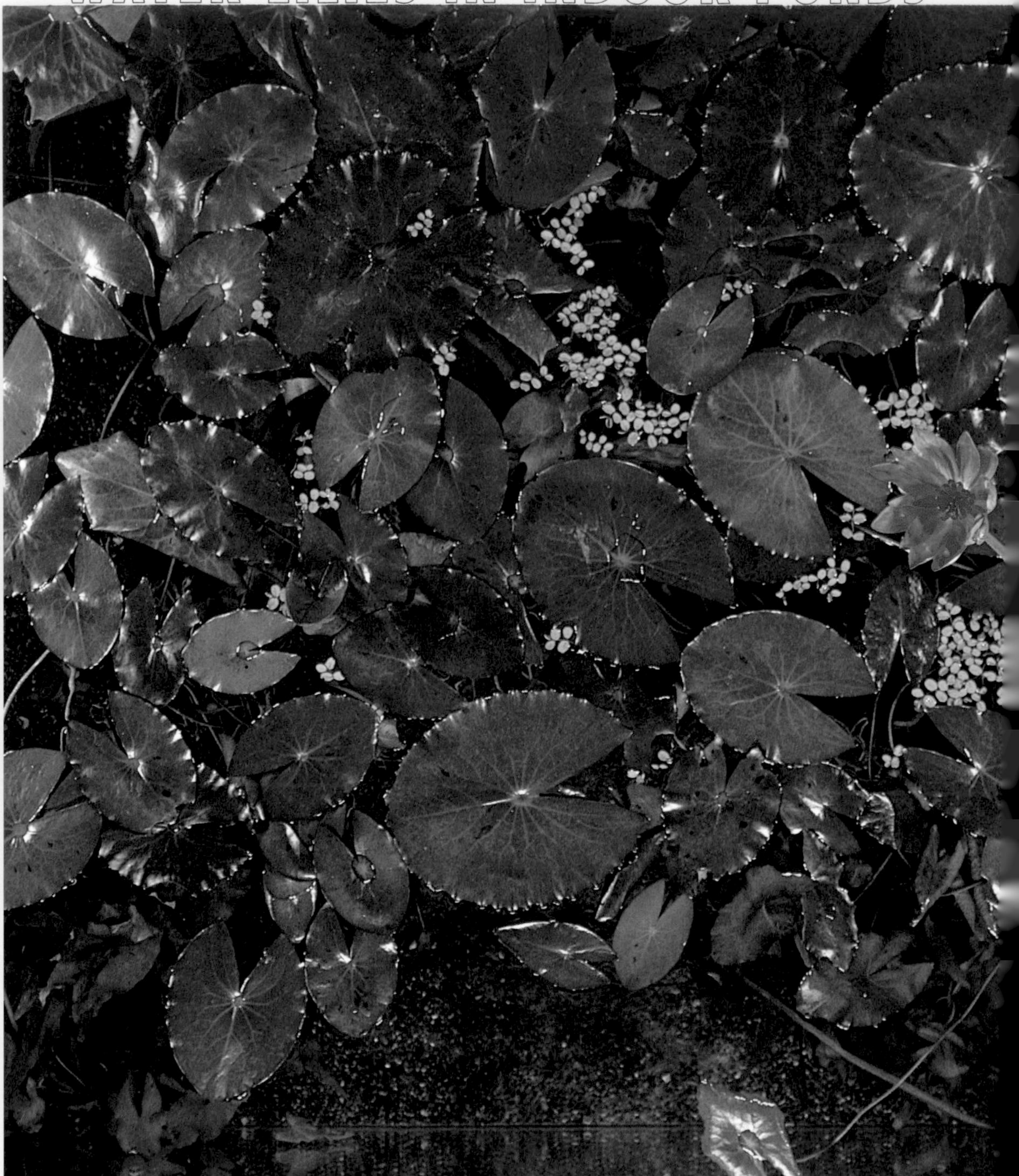

DATA:
*Water temperature*: 27°C (80°F).
*Tank dimensions*: 80 x 80 x 30 cm
                acrylic tank.
*Lighting:* 4 x 20-watt tubes.
*Daily illumination period:* 12 hours.
*Influx of natural light:* None.
*Substrate:* River sand.
*Filtration*: One outside and one inside
filter.
*Water changes:* Up to ⅓ of total
volume once a week.
*Heating:* Two 100-watt heaters,
thermostatically controlled.
*Fertilizer.* Partially mixed into
substrate, suitable supplements  of
liquid fertilizer with each water
change. Addition of carbon dioxide
via diffuser pipe.
*Water quality*: pH 6.5.
*Total hardness:*  4° DH.
*Carbon dioxide in solution:* 8 mg per
liter.

In many regions of Southeast Asia there are water holes and swamps everywhere. We are neither talking about dense jungle growth of tropical trees nor conventional ponds as we find in built-up cities. These water holes and swampy patches are more commonly found in the rural areas along the outskirts of country towns. These are water covered areas with an absolutely calm surface; ponds that are densely covered with the floating leaves of tropical water lilies and where there is no water visible. When we cautiously part the leaves and dare to look into the water below we can see small fishes.

The water temperature tends to climb rather dramatically in these small ponds due to the direct influence of solar radiation during the dry season. The dissolved oxygen level drops correspondingly. The only group of fishes which adapt to such harsh surroundings are the anabantoids, which possess an accessory respiratory organ. The habitat tank described here is to depict this sort of Southeast Asian mood. The principal plants in this tank are numerous *Nymphaea* species because their leaves tend to float on the water surface, conveying the impression of a pond.

In real ponds in Southeast Asia it is difficult to look directly into the water, since the leaves of water lilies cover the entire surface. In our home aquarium we have to avoid such a problem. Therefore, those water lilies with leaves penetrating the surface are planted only in the back of the aquarium. Only bulbs with their first, short leaves still well below the surface, are planted in the foreground. Such a planting arrangement makes it possible to still

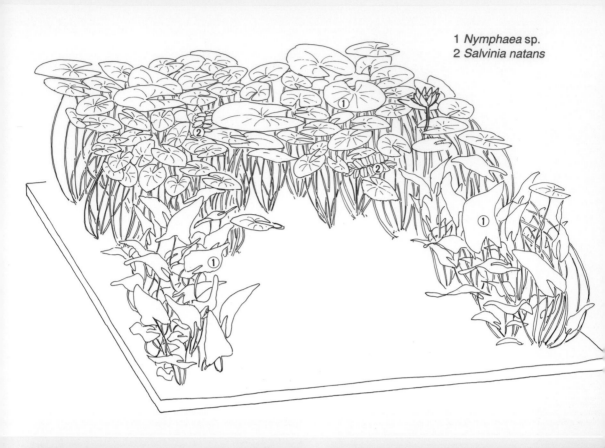

1 *Nymphaea* sp.
2 *Salvinia natans*

*Trichogaster trichopterus*
*Gyrinocheilus aymonieri*

*Trichogaster leeri*
*Trichogaster microlepis*

look down onto the fish.

Driftwood is attached to the back wall of the tank, which gives the tank a greater optical depth. The floating leaves prevent penetration of too much light. This scheme, together with a light water current, is the ideal environment for gouramis of the genera *Trichogaster* and *Colisa.* These fish will spawn more readily in such a tank and their coloration becomes much more intense.

## SETTING UP THE TANK

In order to recreate the atmosphere of a pond, we select a tank with a large bottom area (relative to its height). The tank depicted in the accompanying illustration is an 80 x 80 x 30 cm acrylic tank. For such a habitat tank to appear totally genuine, we should really spread out some mud along the bottom. This, of course, would make substrate maintenance quite difficult. Instead, fine river sand is spread out over the bottom. Since water lilies must not be planted too close together, it is not necessary for the entire substrate to have fertilizer mixed in. During the flowering season these indoor water lilies must be given some direct sunlight, because in order to bring these plants to flower they require a specific amount of light. If need be, the available light intensity and volume can be further enhanced with supplementary artificial illumination (e.g. mercury vapor lamps). Even during the period when the plants are flowering the entire tank should be exposed to an even light volume. If properly maintained, such a special habitat aquarium will easily be the center of attraction in a living room or hallway.

## SELECTING THE PLANTS

For the initial set-up of such an aquarium we purchase germinating bulbs (with sprouts) of different water lily species. Adult plants easily dry up when they are transplanted. Within two to four weeks the new bulbs will develop many new leaves which are still below the water surface but quickly develop into the typical and attractive floating water lily leaves. For this reason it is advisable to plant the water lilies in the back and those at the front at different times. Starting with the back, as soon as those plants have developed a lot of underwater leaves, the bulbs for the foreground are planted. This then creates an aquascape where the leaves in the back are floating on the surface, while those in the front are still below the surface. For the sprouting bulbs planted along the back of the tank we use forceps to place fertilizer pellets into the surrounding substrate. This

The gouramis in this aquarium are all very peaceful, slow-moving fishes.

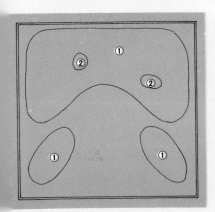

procedure is particularly effective during the flowering season. The plants in the foreground are not fertilized, so they do not develop large floating leaves. Their roots should be cut back with a pair of scissors. The water should be changed regularly as indicated. If the water quality is starting to deviate substantially from the DATA given in the margin of this text, the volume of individual water changes must be reduced; otherwise, the plants will become adversely affected and will wilt.

The inflorescense of the water lily plant, *Nymphaea* sp.

### SELECTING THE FISHES

The fishes of choice for such a tank are small to medium-size gouramis, especially *Trichogaster leeri*, where the males have particularly long fins. Also suitable is *Trichogaster microlepis*, which may be somewhat less active but contributes a significant visual component to this display. *Trichogaster trichopterus*, the blue gourami, is very hardy and easy to breed.

Your local pet shop probably has many kinds of gouramis to offer you as they are now being hybridized.

Gouramis prefer slightly acid, soft water, but since these are very adaptable fish, this is not too important; however, sudden, major changes must be avoided. In essence then, never change very large volumes of water at any one time, since this can easily cause a disease outbreak among the fish.

Gouramis build large bubblenests at the surface. They attach these nests between the plants. Several hundred eggs are deposited at one spawning. These give rise to tiny larvae that are somewhat difficult to rear. Initially these young fish require micro-food, and later on during the activation process of the labyrinth (used in respiration) they need a low water level. Yet, even without stunning breeding success, just observing the entire reproductive process is still very interesting.

**Above:** Dwarf gouramis (*Colisa lalia*) are gentle, peaceful creatures and bear no ill will to any tankmate.
**Below:** *Colisa lalia* variety.

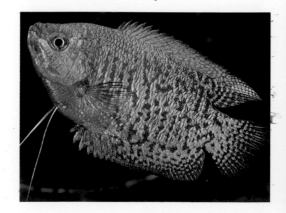

*Trichogaster leeri*, the Pearl Gourami, is one of the most beautiful of all the aquarium fishes. In this planted aquarium, mature males will constantly display their outstanding breeding coloration.

This is an aquarium for barb species from Southeast Asia. Small to medium-size species, such as *Capoeta tetrazona* and *Puntius conchonius* are easy to breed and can provide much pleasure even to beginning aquarists. These generally elegant and attractive barbs are equally popular among experienced aquarists as they are among beginners. But there are some barb species that are less known like *Puntius somphongsi* and *Puntius dorsalis*. Generally, barbs are rarely ever kept in tanks where there are delicate plants, because they tend to feed on them. For that reason barbs are rarely ever found in aquariums with stemmed plants. Plants like *Hygrophila*, for instance, will be

barren within a few days if these fish are hungry. But there are plants, especially those with hard leaves, that can be safely kept with barbs. Plants like *Nymphaea*, *Anubias*, and water ferns are not eaten by *Puntius*, even though these plants have delicate leaves. Apparently they are not very tasty to the fish.

In an aquarium that is intended to display barbs, driftwood roots form the visual and aesthetic center. They give a natural appearance to this aquascape. River sand is a suitable medium as bottom substrate.

One such hardy plant which comes from the same region as *Puntius* is *Microsorium pteropus*. They can be artificially attached to submerged

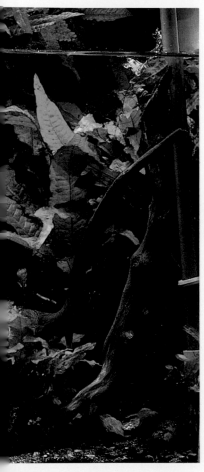

driftwood and onto rocks, where they will quickly become established and continue to grow. Another group of really tough plants that should be planted, are Cryptocorynes. Driftwood and plants form the basis of this habitat aquarium. So that this underwater picture looks as real as possible, we should not introduce too many different species of barbs

The principal species for this kind of aquarium is the Tiger Barb, *Capoeta tetrazona*. In addition, we can use *Puntius conchonius* and *Barbodes everetti*.

The selection of fish species make this a busy tank with lots of colorful action.

DATA:
*Water temperature*: 24° C (75°F).
*Tank dimensions*: 80 x 45 x 45 cm all-glass tank.
*Lighting*: 2 x 20-watt bulbs.
*Daily illumination period:* 15 hours.
*Influx of daylight*: None.
*Substrate:* River sand.
*Filtration:* Outside trickle filter with or without motor drive.
*Water changes*: ⅓ of total volume once per week.
*Heating*: 150-watt heater, thermostatically controlled.
*Fertilizer:* Mixed in with substrate; addition of carbon dioxide is recommended periodically when the plants need a stimulant for growth. Dispense gas via diffuser pipe.
*Water quality*: pH 7.0.
*Total hardness:* 6° DH.
*Carbon dioxide in solution*: 8 mg per liter.

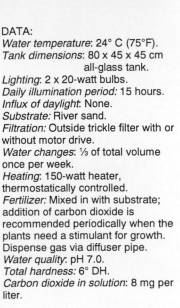

*Capoeta tetrazona*

*Barbodes everetti*

*Puntius conchonius*

*Badis badis*

*Brachygobius doriae*

*Epalzeorhynchus kallopterus*

*Botia striata*

*Botia lohachata*

*Botia macracantha*

1 *Microsorium pteropus*
2 *Hygrophila stricta*
3 *Cryptocoryne wendtii*
4 *Cryptocoryne balansae*
5 *Hygrophila polysperma*
6 *Bolbitis heteroclita*
7 *Ceratopteris cornuta*

## SETTING UP THE TANK

The maximum size of the Southeast Asian *Capoeta tetrazona* and *Puntius conchonius* is 5 to 10 cm. Because these are rather active fish, we should select a tank with a minimum length of 80 cm. The bottom substrate should be river sand. Its small grain size prevents food particles from becoming trapped in the substrate. It is not necessary to fertilize the entire substrate. Instead, fertilizer pellets or tablets are buried only in the vicinity of the Cryptocorynes.

As far as the lighting is concerned, it is sufficient to illuminate an 80 cm tank with two 20-watt lamps. For a 100 cm aquarium we use two 30-watt lamps. If the light is too bright, neither *Microsorium* nor *Cryptocoryne* will grow well. Stemmed plants such as *Hygrophila*, which are to be kept in such an aquarium with a low light level, should be planted directly underneath the light source in order to compensate for the inadequate lighting.

The driftwood lends a certain natural appearance to such an aquarium. With it we can also create steps in the substrate. Java Fern does very well in a tank like this.

## SELECTING THE PLANTS

We select plants and fishes that come from the same geographical regions. Among Southeast Asian plants there are many different species, from soft-leafed *Rotala macrantha* to *Microsorium* with its firm leaves. Since the leaves of submerged stemmed plants are usually very tender, they represent a highly acceptable food for the barb species. Similarly, *Cryptocoryne* would also be suitable, but they too are eaten by barbs. Java Fern, with its really firm leaves, is planted in the center of the tank. It has an important role to play in the stabilization of the tank water. During routine tank maintenance the Java Fern should be thinned out, so that it does not grow too densely; this way, the driftwood also remains visible. *Cryptocoryne* grows in groups, but even in such an arrangement they are gradually decimated by the barbs.

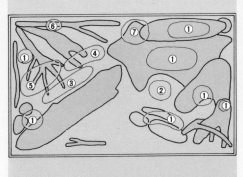

When you trim back your plants, remember to remove the clippings so they don't rot in the tank and adversely affect your water quality.

## SELECTING THE FISH

From among the small to medium-size barbs, we select only those species that are very attractive, for instance, the well-known Tiger Barb, *Capoeta tetrazona*. *Puntius conchonius*, the Rosy Barb, develops its full beauty only when fully grown. *Barbodes everetti,* the Clown Barb, with its attractive red-yellow-black-contrasting pattern is also one of the more attractive barbs. Ideal companions for barbs are *Botia* loaches, which inhabit the lower regions of the aquarium. There are many different species, but most of them are of a somewhat dubious disposition. When they are put together with relatively peaceful fishes there can be difficulties. Among the barbs, however, there are no problems. Moreover, there are a few *Botia* species that are relatively calm, like *Botia lohachata* and *Botia macracantha,* the clown loach.

As far as the water quality is concerned, neither the *Botia* nor the barbs are particularly demanding. If the water is really clean, the barbs can even be bred in this tank. The Java Fern will grow very well in this tank, provided regular partial water changes are being made.

The Clown Loach (*Botia macracantha*) is aptly named. These endearing little busybodies will provide endless amusement as they dive and roll throughout the tank.

Both photos on this page are of the Tiger Barb (*Capoeta tetrazona*), but of different varieties.

DATA:
*Water temperature:* 25°C (77°F).
*Tank dimensions:* 100 x 45 x 45 cm (40 x 18 x 18 in.) all-glass tank.
*Lighting:* 2 x 20-watt lamps.
*Daily illumination period:* 12 hours.
*Influx of daylight:* Up to midday.
*Substrate:* Very fine gravel.
*Filtration:* External filter.
*Water changes:* ⅓ of total volume once every two weeks.
*Heating:* 150-watt heater, thermostatically-controlled.
*Fertilizer:* None.
*Water quality:* pH 7.0.
*Total hardness:* 10° DH.

If we want to adequately accommodate fishes that come from the steamy jungle regions and mangrove swamps of Southeast Asia, we have to duplicate a mangrove landscape in the aquarium.

Mangrove roots exhibit a highly specialized form of growth. They wrap themselves around trees. Mangroves live in the framework of soft swamps. These aerial roots grow like the tentacles of a polyp. They are extremely dense. When the lagoons and swamps are submerged during the flood, the aerial roots of mangroves will also disappear UNDER the water. This is NOT quite the way it is. These are NOT mangroves that are being described. Mangroves basically are tidal trees that thrive between fresh

The Archerfish (*Toxotes jaculator*) is well-known for its ability to knock insects into the range by spitting a jet of water.

water and marine water flooding. They do attract many brackish water fishes and they do make an interesting aquascape. There is no exact word in English for a fresh water mangrove swamp.

Many fishes, in search of food, will gather in this mangrove forest during the flood. They are marine fishes that can also tolerate brackish water, and so they enter river deltas close to the ocean. There are also freshwater fishes that live in the lower reaches of rivers. The fish that can be found there is highly variable. Species of marine gobies, *Scatophagus argus*, Archerfish (*Toxotes jaculator*), *Monodactylus argenteus*, and others live there. True brackish water fishes do very well under these conditions. The submersed roots of the mangroves provide excellent hiding places.

Since the aerial roots of real mangroves can easily be damaged when they are submerged, we do not use them at all in this aquarium. Instead, we use long, thin "finger-like" pieces of driftwood and secure these to a black sheet of acrylic with the lower ends projecting into the aquarium (see illustration) like roots. Since the roots of true mangroves are rather large, we reduce the scale, so the aesthetic appearance conforms to the size of the fishes as well as to the tank dimensions. In the section above the water surface we simulate leaves of true mangroves. For instance, a *Ficus bengalensis* would enhance the atmosphere nicely, but unfortunately it is too large for an aquarium such as this one. Therefore, we use leafy plants from the same geographical region. The submerged part of the aquarium, and where there are no plants at all, should be covered to prevent excessive evaporation.

## SETTING UP THE AQUARIUM

The size of the aquarium must always reflect the size of fish to be

1 *Sissus* sp.
2 *Cordyline terminalis*
3 *Pandanus* sp.
4 *Fontinalis antipyretica*

*Toxotes jaculator*
*Cynoglossus* sp.

*Scatophagus argus*
*Chanda ranga*

*Periophthalmus*
*Tetraodon fluviatilis*

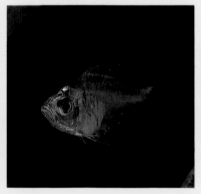

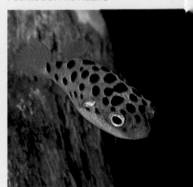

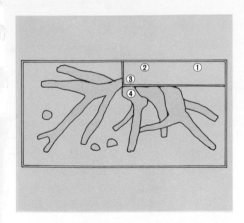

kept in it. If, for instance, the fishes are about 5 cm long, a small aquarium is adequate. Archerfish, however, will grow in excess of 10 cm and so require a larger tank. The driftwood used to simulate mangrove roots becomes the principal exhibit component. Suitable and thoroughly cleaned driftwood pieces are available from most aquarium shops. It is not advisable to collect your own roots, since they are probably not sufficiently dried out and will quickly start to get moldy and spoil the water. Black acrylic panels are used to which the roots are attached. They have to be fastened in such a way that they depict the position and shape of mangrove roots. The acrylic panels are placed on the aquarium bottom, and from there the roots "grow" upward. This method gives the roots a secure hold because they are resting on the acrylic sheets. These are available from various dealers trading in plastic, PVC, and acrylic panels. The wood pieces are cut to size with a saw, and holes are drilled into the acrylic sheets. The individual pieces of wood are then attached to the sheets by means of (stainless steel) screws.

It is important to let the wood appear to be intertwined in a complex shape, so that it looks like a mangrove root. To create a swampy environment

we spread very fine-grained gravel over the bottom; gravel is important if fish are going to be bred in this tank. For this reason it is also important that the water is slightly alkaline and hard. At the top of this root structure we secure some soil together with the leafy plants (see illustration). The acrylic sheets with the "roots" attached are positioned on the bottom in such a way that the soil at the top does not become immersed in the tank water. The acrylic sheet, which controls the position of the roots, is placed on the bottom of the aquarium.

Filtration is by means of a canister filter. To maintain the hard and alkaline water conditions, we can mix some coral sand in with the gravel.

Don't forget the Malawi/Tanganyika salts with this selection of fishes. Brackish water is necessary to keep them in good health.

Lighting has to be arranged in such a way that the light reaches the water—the space between the roots as well as the plants.

### SELECTING THE FISHES

Fishes for this aquarium have to be selected from among the Southeast Asian "brackish water" fishes. The illustrations accompanying this text contain photos of *Toxotes jaculator*, which displays quite an extraordinary feeding behavior, and *Periophthalmus barbarus*, the famous mudskipper. Other brackish water fishes that should not be absent from a mangrove aquarium include the small freshwater Puffer, *Tetraodon fluviatilis*, *Monodactylus argenteus*, the Mono, and *Scatophagus argus*, the Scat, which all look like marine fish. Finally, we can also include the freshwater Sole, which tends to bury itself in the fine gravel, where it is barely visible because of its excellent camouflage coloration. None of the fishes live in pure freshwater. Therefore, the water needs to be adjusted to conform to the normal environment of these species by making it slightly saline. Normally we mix fresh water in with salt water at a ratio of 3:1. To accomplish this requires about 8 to 10 grams of sea salt per liter of freshwater.

The fishes will easily adapt to the new aquarium conditions. When they are in good condition it is possible to breed them in water with a lower salt concentration. So that they are gradually being adapted, we use mainly fresh water for the partial water changes. This then gradually dilutes the salt concentration. It is, however, important to keep in mind that these specimens must not be transferred directly into fresh water. It can happen that certain species, like the Archerfish, will turn dark and eventually die. Should the fish show signs of stress, a small amount of salt is added to the water again. Partial water changes should be made every 14 days. On these occasions we must not forget add the salt supplement.

Puffers are feisty little fellows. They have impressive teeth and will rid a tank of snails in no time.

**Above:** Scats need some salt in their water to lead long and healthy lives.
**Right:** Archerfish *(Toxotes jaculator)* are very impressive when they reach full maturity. Like the Scats, they need to be kept in brackish water.

# EAST
# &
# WEST
# AFRICA

## WEST AFRICAN RIVERS

Habitat tanks featuring fishes and water plants from West Africa have become particularly popular during the last few years. In general it is quite acceptable when using *Anubias* as principal plants, to combine the monochrome of these plants with *Nymphaea lotus, Crinum* and *Bolbitis*. In tanks set up solely with *Anubias*, aesthetically pleasing depth is lacking when the plants are placed only in the substrate. If, however, these plants are growing on rocks and driftwood, their leaves will eventually form dense growth that gives rise to a magical picture. In this setup, *Anubias nana* is the main plant. Long-leafed *Anubias afzelii* and

*Anubias congensis* are planted at the optical intersections. Even in a superbly decorated aquarium, its visual impact is reduced by using plants that have their leaves protruding above the surface. The principal elements of this display, the *Anubias nana*, will give a certain optical depth to this aquarium. In addition, we need to use at least one long-leafed *Anubias* to create a contrast in the open swimming space. There, we can also see structures made up of real rocks, which give the impression of an African atmosphere. The *Anubias* are planted together just like stemmed plants. On one side there is the luxuriant growth of the common *Anubias nana*. Young

DATA:
*Water temperature:* 26°C (79F).
*Tank dimensions:* 80 x 50 x 40 cm (30 x 18 x 16 in.) acrylic tank.
*Lighting:* 2 x 20-watt lamps.
*Daily illumination period:* 12 hours.
*Influx of daylight:* None.
*Substrate:* Coarse river sand.
*Filtration:* Canister filter.
*Heating:* 1 x 200-watt thermostatic heater.
*Water changes:* Irregularly, however, at least ¼ of the tank volume every 14 days.
*Fertilizer:* None.
*Water quality:* pH 6.9.
*Total hardness:* 6° DH.
*Carbon dioxide in solution:* 10 mg per liter.

This little catfish will not damage the plants, but will perform a valuable service in cleaning algae off the leaves.

runners of *Anubias congensis* are sprouting in the foreground. Slightly off center we have *Anubias afzelii* and to the the other side we plant *Anubias nana*, which tends to grow fairly large and then displays its green leaves in hair-like waves. We use up to 50 plants of *Anubias nana*, two *Anubias afzelii*, 12 *Anubias congensis* and three *Anubias barteri* var. *angustifolia*.

## SETTING UP THE TANK

It is easy to create optical depth if the available aquarium is deep. Coarse river sand is ideal as a substrate for such a tank. Soil fertilizer should only be used where there are *Anubias* planted. We select a few nicely shaped rocks. For *Anubias* tanks we must not use driftwood or rocks that are light red. This would render the entire picture unnatural. In order to enhance the dark green of the water plants and to develop a natural atmosphere, ash-grey to dark grey rocks are more suitable as is red or blackish-brown driftwood. Before we start decorating the tank we tie a number of *Anubias nana* to a piece of wood. A rubber band is ideal for attaching the plants to the piece of wood.

With *Anubias* species it is common for the roots to grow horizontally. This must be taken into consideration when attaching the

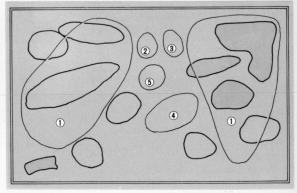

*Phenacogrammus interruptus*

*Pelvicachromis subocellatus*

plants, i.e. there must be sufficient space left between adjacent plants. Water plants arranged in this manner create a virtual *Anubias* forest.

## SELECTING THE PLANTS

To purchase a large number of *Anubias* at one time is rather expensive. Instead, we wait for natural reproduction to take place. Of

1 *Anubias nana*
2 *Anubias afzelii*
3 *Anubias barteri var. angustifolia*
4 *Anubias congoensis*
5 *Anubias lanceolata*

The *Anubias* will fill in very nicely given proper conditions and a little time.

course, initially such an aquarium looks a bit spartan. Those plants that are to grow on driftwood are initially the important ones.

Since it takes a while for new roots to develop, some of the plants can initially also be placed in the substrate in order to develop roots there. After that, they are transferred to appropriate pieces of driftwood. *Anubias* species do not require particular care. A single 20-watt lamp is sufficient for a 60 cm long tank. For a 90 cm long tank we use two 20-watt lamps. If a bit of algae develops on the leaves, the cause lies in the filter. Either it is clogged or the substrate has become an aerobic, or both. The algae is taken off the leaves by hand and the substrate and the filter must be cleaned out.

## SELECTING THE FISHES

An ideal match for the dark green *Anubias* are fishes that have more of a subdued beauty rather than a conspicuous coloration. A good combination are West-African Congo Tetras, *Phenacogrammus interruptus*, which keep themselves in mid-water. This species can be nicely complemented with dwarf cichlids like *Nanochromis* and *Pelvicachromis*, which tend to remain near the bottom.

*Phenacogrammus* are available throughout the year from most major aquarium shops. Even when buying sub-adult or juvenile specimens, these will grow rapidly into beautiful fish when given a proper diet. If they are not being fed enough, their teeth marks will be visible on the tough *Anubias* leaves.

*Pelvicachromis* and *Nanochromis* are not always available throughout the year. Especially *Pelvicachromis taeniatus*, should be purchased as soon as an opportunity to do so arises, since this species is usually fairly rare.

West African cichlids are very prone to diseases when the water quality deteriorates. Regular water changes and cleanliness of the filtration unit are essential in order to prevent these diseases. It is important not to overcrowd the tank!

*Nanochromis parilus* are not always easy to find, so snatch them up when you do see them. It helps if you let your dealer know you are interested, so he can alert you when they appear on the wholesalers' lists.

**Above:** The sight of a school of Congo Tetras is not soon forgotten. The iridescent scales show up best in natural sunlight. **Below:** A pair of *Pelvicachromis pulcher* prior to spawning.

DATA:
*Water temperature:* 24°C (75°F).
*Air temperature:* 26°C (79°F).
*Tank dimensions:* 60 x 50 x 50 cm (24 x 20 x 20 in.) acrylic tank.
*Lighting:* 3 x 20-watt lamps.
*Daily illumination period:* 12 hours.
*Influx of daylight:* None.
*Substrate:* Coarse river sand.
*Filtration:* Combination of substrate filter and canister filter.
*Water changes:* Irregular, depending upon condition of fishes.
*Heating:* Room (ambient) heating and tank illumination.
*Fertilizer:* None.
*Water quality:* pH 6.9.
*Total hardness:* 4° DH.
*Carbon dioxide in solution:* 8 mg per liter.

Many aquatic plants will flower under aquarium conditions when their leaves grow out of the water.

This habitat tank represents an attempt to depict the jungle banks of West African rivers and their upper reaches with *Anubias* and *Bolbitis* that have become attached to rocky platforms, the large leaves of *Barteri*, which penetrate the water surface close to the river bank, and so on. When looking at photographs of those areas where there are naturally occurring *Anubias* stands we discover many different and interesting things. The rocks and boulders are dark grey and the plants look as if they had been glued into the cracks and crevices. These areas are distinctly different from those of the Amazon River and Southeast Asia. It is more like a landscape that is reminiscent of mountain streams.

Plants that have grown onto the rocks in the river, various types of ferns that poke their faces out of the water, and dense forests which continue endlessly beyond the water are scenes that can be found in West Africa.

A West African terrarium is distinguished from a standard terrarium where the back section is separated off with terrestrial plants. Most plants are here under water. By regulating the water level we can also simulate the rainy season as well as the dry season. In a water patch, hidden behind the large leaves of an *Anubias*, *Pantodon* are fluttering about and among the dark cavities of rock piles *Synodontis* are sleeping. The cute *Gnathonemus*, which has paused momentarily, is waiting for the hours of darkness.

1 *Anubias lanceolata*
2 *Bolbitis heudelotii*
3 *Anubias barteri var. barteri*
4 *Anubias auliclata*
5 *Anubias nana*
6 *Fontinalis antipyretica*

*Pantodon buchholzi*
*Synodontis nigriventris*

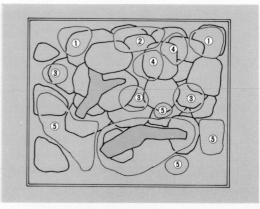

## SETTING UP THE TANK

When setting up this tank, emphasis must be placed on the arrangement of stones and river sand, and so it is advisable to do this work more diligently than when working with plants. I start with the rocks. In the upper reaches of rivers there are differently colored and shaped formations. To set a West African scene, preference should be given to smooth rocks. Rounded off rocks, like smooth-cornered cubes, are ideal for constructing the rock formations. The height of this display is just as important as for an *Anubias* terrarium. The minimum height is about 45 cm. The tall-growing *Anubias* will soon grow beyond the edge of the tank and will become scorched and wilted by the heat of the tank illumination.

The rock formations are constructed sequentially from the back forward, rock by rock. The rocks are placed on top of each other at different angles so that adjacent rock piles essentially interface. Particularly attractive rocks are used to correct the overall appearance and are also used in the foreground of the tank. When the rock formations are almost complete, we fill the gaps between the rocks with plants. *Anubias* will develop bizarre-looking roots among the rocks. Even though this is a water plant display, the long-leafed *Anubias* species and the *Bolbitis* must be arranged behind the rock formations, since their fast-growing leaves protrude above the surface. At the optical intersection we position individual, especially decorative plants.

As soon as the display has been completed, the return flow from the canister filter is discharged over the plants (possibly using a spray bar). This method facilitates water evaporation and so increases the humidity in the tank. *Anubias*, especially, will wilt easily if they do not get enough moisture. It is also important that the tanks's cover glass fit tightly.

We can plant *Fontinalis*, mosses, and ferns from mountain streams on and around the wet rocks. If there is good growth, their delicate leaves will cover all the rocks. The *Bolbitis* and the African fern are attached with cotton threads to small stones, which are then placed on or among the rocks. As soon as they start to grow, they will spread in all directions.

## FISH AND PLANT SELECTION

We have to be careful with *Bolbitis*, the Congo Water Fern. Its leaves will immediately wilt when exposed to air. The filter is important for circulating water so that it enhances the condition of the substrate. By using a spray bar on the filter, we create an artificial rain-shower effect. This keeps the *Anubias* wet. The water should be changed every 14 days. As far as the fish are concerned, we select those that appeal to us. Small species, such as *Pantodon buchholzi*, *Gnathonemus petersii*, and *Synodontis nigriventris*, are very suitable for this sort of tank. If it is possible to use a larger tank, we can then select a greater variety of fish.

In any event, we must make sure that all fish specimens selected are healthy, since with a smaller tank volume the water quality can deteriorate quite rapidly, and it is difficult to remove any fish from the tank once they are in it.

Peter's Elephantnose (*Gnathonemus* sp.) will spend its time searching the substrate for small worms. Make sure the gravel has no sharp edges that could damage its lower appendage.

Malawi cichlids are highly territorial. Be sure there are plenty of caves in the rockwork.

DATA:
*Water temperature:* 26°C (79°F).
*Tank dimensions:* 120 x 45 x 45 cm

*Lighting:* 4 x 20-watt lamps.
*Daily illumination period:* 12 hours.
*Influx of natural light:* Indirect sunlight for a few hours every day. Be careful not to overheat the tank or create an algae problem.
*Substrate:* River sand and gravel at a ratio of 2:1.
*Filtration:* External filter.
*Water changes:* ⅓ of tank volume every 14 days.
*Heater:* 200-watt heater automatically controlled.
*Fertilizer:* None.
*Water quality:* pH 7.8.
*Total hardness:* 12° DH.

This is a habitat tank for Lake Malawi cichlids. When looking at a photograph taken in the natural habitat of these fish we see the shapes of active fish. The sandy bottom is covered with rubble and

sparsely covered with algae. Here we find a multitude of fishes, with colors that glow like those of marine fish. This is an area where giant rocky cliffs protrude from the shore into the water, creating a somewhat desolate scene, and where there seems to be a vast sandy region along the bottom. This is the habitat of the active and attractive *Pseudotropheus, Copadichromis, Nimbochromis, Sciaenochromis, Protomelas*, and *Aulonocara* species. This rocky aquascape is the model for this habitat aquarium. Among the fish mentioned above—the main occupants of this tank—there are a number of species that grow rather large. Therefore, if we do not include large rocks in the decor for this tank, the dynamic atmosphere of the lake cannot be depicted properly. The small rocks in the lake can have diameters of up to 2 or 3 meters. It is,

of course, impossible to have rocks like that in an aquarium. Therefore, we are trying to depict a miniature version of Lake Malawi using relatively small rocks. Although we are talking here about relatively large rocks, we still have to take care that the aesthetic balance of this tank is not upset. We also use many small and medium rocks, which fit harmoniously together with the larger rocks.

## SETTING UP THE TANK

The tank should be as large as possible because the fishes reach maximum sizes of 10 to 20 cm. Moreover, they have a tendency to defend their territories aggressively. The tank shown in the accompanying illustration is 120 cm long, which is essentially the minimum size required for the type of display discussed here. Since this is a display where many

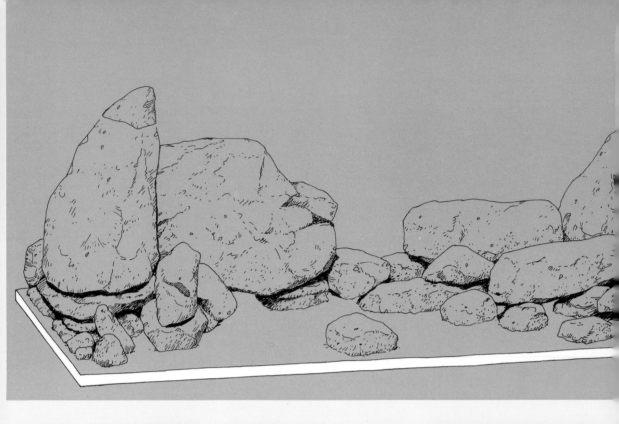

*Sciaenochromis fryeri*
*Aulonocara jacobfreibergi*

*Aulonocara maylandi*
*Nimbochromis fuscotaeniatus*

*Protomelas taeniolatus*
*Copadichromis chrysonotus*

Rock work in this tank has been set up to accommodate various Lake Malawi species.

is in an area without sunlight, we need to install four 20-watt fluorescent tubes.

## SELECTING THE FISHES

Fish selection can be left to individual tastes and preferences. Specimen size and numbers are, of course, dependent upon the size of the tank chosen. These cichlids establish territories and they have a well-defined breeding behavior. Detailed instructions with regard to care and breeding can be obtained from relevant aquarium handbooks. The TFH book *Ad Koning's Book of Cichlids and All Other Fishes of Lake Malawi (TS-157)* is by far the best book on the subject. All fishes selected for this tank should be introduced at the same time.

rocks are being used, an acrylic tank, which does not break as easily, is more appropriate than an all-glass tank. The entire bottom area needs to be covered with a layer of Styrofoam®, about 1 cm thick. This prevents the bottom from being damaged.

The color shades of the rocks to be used are medium to dark grey. The shape of the rocks should be cubic and without sharp edges. Before water is put into the tank, the rock formations should be constructed. First the lay the foundation with large rocks. Medium and small rocks are placed more towards the front. The optical depth of the aquarium is emphasized if the large rocks are in the back and the small ones toward the front. Since the arrangement of rock formations determines the aesthetic appeal of this tank, much attention needs to be paid to this aspect. In order to further enhance the beautiful coloration of the fishes, a high light intensity is required. Of course, sun light would be ideal, however, this would create the risk of excessive algae growth. If this tank

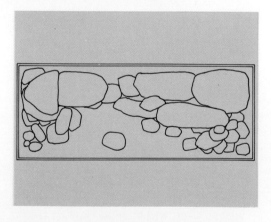

Specimens added later on are usually severely suppressed or even killed. The sex ratio should be arranged so that there are several females for every male. Smaller specimens are often weakened by the aggressive behavior of larger ones.

Fishes from Lake Malawi required hard and slightly alkaline water. The pH value should not drop below 7.0. Extensive water changes with soft water must be avoided. Artificial hardening of water is possible using Lake Malawi salts. These salts are available from your pet shop. Do NOT add sea salt!

Here we are trying to represent a West African aquascape in a large tank. The term "West African aquascape" refers to a habitat tank where the aesthetic appearance is determined by the lance-shaped leaves of many *Anubias* plants.

*Anubias* grow along the banks of many West African rivers, but they rarely ever occur in water. Even those plants close to the water will merely extend their leaves onto the water where they will spread out. In this tank we do not necessarily have to use *Anubias*. In our demonstration tank, an attempt was made to reconstruct the streambeds of West African rivers. It is important to create a natural atmosphere. That is the reason for floating leaves of *Nymphaea lotus*. The long leaves of *Crinum natans* are not to be trimmed. In the shadow of these leaves, that is, in areas where there is only subdued light, we plant *Bolbitis huedelotii*, the Congo water fern.

Large rocks and driftwood are the optical focal points in this habitat aquarium. The rocks, which create a

somewhat West African mood, are specifically selected for that purpose. In order to set the scene of a natural West African habitat, we need to use rocks of a certain size. Their surface must look attractive and they must not be hidden under plants. The driftwood, too, should be large and, if possible, represent a swamp. In setting up this tank we start with the large components, so that their shapes and configurations look appropriate.

There are many species of water plants that originate in West Africa. Those plants belonging to the same species are planted together. In contrast to the large plants, we should select small fish species, since these combinations occur quite often in nature and in small rivers where water plants grow.

For the upper reaches we select African *Aplocheilichthys normani*, for the middle water layers *Hemigrammopetersius caudalis*, and for the bottom of the tank *Nanochromis transvestitus* and *Pelvicachromis taeniatus*. This is a

# LANDSCAPE

DATA
*Water temperature:* 25°C (77°F).
*Tank dimensions:* 100 x 45 x 45 cm (40 x 18 x 18 in.).
*Lighting:* 2 x 20-watt lamps.
*Daily illumination period:* 12 hours.
*Influx of daylight:* Up to midday exposure to diffused sunshine.
*Substrate:* Very fine gravel.
*Filtration:* External filter.
*Water changes:* ¼ of total volume once every two weeks.
*Heating:* 150-watt heater, thermostatically-controlled.
*Fertilizer:* None.
*Water quality:* pH 7.0.
*Total hardness:* 10° DH.

combination which takes into consideration the natural swimming levels of particular species in an aquarium.

Lampeyes, so called for their large, luminous eyes, are escape artists and should have a secure cover on their aquarium.

## SETTING UP THE TANK

We use the largest possible tank with a minimum length of 100 cm. In view of the large rocks being used, an acrylic tank is more suitable than an all-glass tank. This lessens the danger of the glass bottom panel breaking. In those sites where large

Pelvicachromis taeniatus
Nanochromis transvestitus

Aplocheilichthys normani
Barbus callipterus

1 *Nymphaea lotus* green
2 *Bolbitis huedelotii*
3 *Crinum natans*
4 *Nymphaea lotus* red

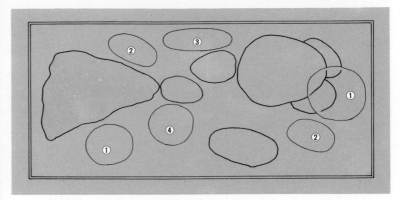

especially becomes weakened when transferred to another site. This rather large-growing African plant can be transplanted only with considerable difficulty, since a mature plant has an extraordinarily large number of roots. If these roots are cut back before planting they will regrow poorly. The same applies to the green tiger lotus, *Nymphaea lotus*.

Plants that are in an advanced state of germination and where there are already the beginnings of white root threads, are most suitable. It is important not to damage the roots while placing them into the substrate. *Bolbitis* will grow on rocks when properly secured to the rock with a rubber band. *Bolbitis* prefers water that is slightly acidic and of medium hardness. If the water current in this tank is increased, black roots will develop and become firmly attached to the rocks. For *Bolbitis* it is important that the water be aged for proper growth. For this reason, we do without frequent water changes in this habitat tank. It is perfectly adequate to exchange about one-fourth of the water every two weeks.

rocks are to be positioned, we place a sheet of Styrofoam® on the bottom of the tank. As a substrate we use a uniformly grained river sand. If we use *Crinum*, it is imperative that the layer of substrate be sufficiently thick. Large and small stones are stacked into a step-like arrangement. So that the substrate sand does not pour through the cracks between adjacent rocks, we block them off with small pebbles. If possible, we use halogen or mercury vapor lamps for illumination. When using fluorescent tubes, these need to be installed directly above the plants. *Bolbitis* does not require special lighting. A large-capacity inside filter can be used for filtration.

## SELECTING THE PLANTS

Apart from *Bolbitis*, it is advisable to purchase plants which are not yet fully developed; *Crinum natans*

## SELECTING THE FISHES

There are many aquarium fish species that live in small rivers in West Africa. A species that remains in the upper water regions is the very beautiful Lampeye, *Aplocheilichthys normani*. For the middle water layers we select the medium-sized *Hemigrammopetersius caudalis*, which is placid and very attractive. The bottom can be inhabited by juvenile *Nanochromis transvestitus* and *Pelvicachromis taeniatus*. For these fishes to remain healthy, regular partial water changes must be maintained. Proper filtration is also essential for the well-being of the fishes.

**Above:** *Aplocheilichthys spilauchen* are prone to jumping. Be sure you cover the tank! **Facing page:** *Phlenacogrammus interruptus,* the Congo Tetra.

This tank depicts a reconstruction of rocky regions in Lake Tanganyika, the home of many cichlids. The cichlids of Lake Tanganyika are all differentiated from each other in peculiar ways. *Pierre Brichard's Book of Cichlids and Other Fishes of Lake Tanganyika* (TS-116) is wonderful, and you are advised to consult it for further information about the hundreds of cichlids found in this very deep lake. Lake Tanganyika, just like Lake Malawi, also has various distinct habitats. Here, too, are regions where rocky shores continue on into the water. There are other areas where there are vast rock and rubble accumulations, and yet again, other areas with dense plant growth.

For the example given here we have chosen very interesting rock zones, the habitat of *Julidochromis* and *Neolamprologus*.

If an attempt is made to represent a Lake Tanganyika scene in an aquarium, we must construct rock formations by stacking large and small rocks on top of each other; however, when doing this we also create something that does look very similar to Lake Malawi. The entire habitat display consists of miniature rock piles, which attract these cichlids. For this purpose, we use limestone-like rock. Since *Julidochromis* like to spawn on overhanging rocks it is advisable to leave sufficient gaps between

DATA:
*Water temperature*: 26°C (79°F).
*Tank dimensions*: 100 x 45 x 45 cm (40 x 18 x 18 in.) all-glass tank.
*Lighting*: 1 x 30-watt lamp.
*Daily illumination period:* 10 hours.
*Influx of daylight*: None.
*Substrate*: River sand and gravel.
*Filtration:* Inside filter.
*Water changes:* About ¼ of tank volume once a week.
*Heating:* 100-watt heater thermostatically controlled.
*Fertilizer:* None.
*Water quality*: pH 8.0.
*Total hardness:* 15° DH.

adjacent rocks. This creates a labyrinth-like structure.

In contrast the Lake Malawi display, we use angular rocks here. This assures greater structural stability to the rock formations so they do not collapse.

To assure that breeding takes place, we need—in addition to limestone rocks—also slightly alkaline and hard water. This can be aided by the use of Lake Malawi/Tanganyika salts that your pet shop can supply.

Since these cichlids tend to maintain their individual territories, the rock formations have to be positioned in such a way that the fish can readily delineate their territories.

Don't be surprised if you find that you have several generations of fry growing up with their parents in this tank.

A tank set up for Lake Tanganyika species.

*Julidochromis regani*
*Neolamprologus leleupi*

*Lamprichthys tanganicanus*
*Neolamprologus cylindricus*

*Telmatochromis temporalis*
*Neolamprologus pulcher*

Don't be afraid to add the special Malawi/Tanganyika salts to the water. The fish really need the additional minerals, carbonates, and trace elements.

Those pairs which have found a suitable territory will no doubt reproduce quite readily. They will also be very protective of their territory.

## SETTING UP THE TANK

The tank must be at least 80 cm long. A larger bottom area will reduce territorially-inspired aggression. Tank depth (front to back) is more important than tank height. The rocks must be of limestone. Large pieces are chiseled down to the required size and shape. The entire bottom panel is covered with a sheet of Styrofoam®, just as we have done for the Lake Malawi tank. Similarly, we also construct the rock formations before the tank is filled with water. The structural foundation should be flat rocks, upon which we place small, cube-shaped rocks, and again flat rocks on top. We also use the back wall of the tank to support these rock formations. In the space between the rocks and the back of the tank we also place a sheet of Styrofoam®, and the rocks are piled against it in a terrace-like fashion with small, protruding cliffs.

As soon as the rock formations have been completed, thoroughly washed sand is spread over the tank bottom. The consists of half river sand and the other half small gravel.

This is a good approximation of the light sand color in Lake Tanganyika.

As far as tank location and lighting is concerned, the same applies here as listed for the Lake Malawi tank. If possible, the tank should be located so that it is exposed to some daylight.

## SELECTING THE FISHES

The focus of attention is on small- to medium-size *Julidochromis* and *Neolamprologus*. The illustration shows a mixture of intensely yellow *N. pulcher* "Daffodil," the relatively recently imported *N. cylindricus*, *N. brevis* and *N. ocellatus* "Yellow," together with the relatively large *N. sexfasciatus*. In their native habitats nearly all of these fish live in lower or middle water regions; they show the same behavior in an aquarium. Since this would make the upper water regions look fairly desolate we add *Lamprichthys tanganicanus*. This species frequents the upper and middle water layers in an aquarium and so it presents a nice contrast to *Neolamprologus*. Fishes from Lake Tanganyika should be given very alkaline and hard water. They are rather sensitive to sudden changes in water condition, and so water changes should be small and frequent.

# INDEX